CHAPTER 28: "The Book Flea market, by the writer, in Raleigh, North Carolina. Jeannie is Jean Shafer of Cary, North Carolina and she really is a family bookstore manager.

CHAPTER 29: The Big House is a part of The Cape Fear Historical Complex located in Fayetteville, North Carolina.

CHAPTER 30: The sheep were photographed at a sheep farm in Willow Springs, North Carolina.

CHAPTER 31: The three crosses were a part of a yard display at a church in Garner, North Carolina. "The Light of the World" banner was photographed during a puppet show in Mebane, North Carolina.

The Ol' Cowpoke

Sez **Howdy**

TO FRANCINE
I'VE HEARD A LOT
ABOUT YOU.
YOUR ARE A BLESSING
TO MORE THAN YOU KNOW
REMEMBER JESUS LOVES
YOU AND WE DO TOO.
THE OL' COWPOKE
MISS JANE

The Ol' Cowpoke Sez Howdy

W. Odell Mann

Dageforde Publishing, Inc.

ISBN: 1-886225-92-3

Cover design by Angie Johnson.

Scripture quotations marked KJV or KJ are from the Authorized King James Version.

Scripture quotations marked NKV are from the Authorized New King James Version.

Scripture quotations marked NASV are from the Authorized New American Standard Version.

Scripture quotations marked LB are from the Living Bible.

Any similarity to any person living or dead, any event either in print or otherwise is purely accidental and not by purpose does the author wish to reflect any remembrance in any manner whatsoever.

Dageforde Publishing, Inc.
128 East 13th Street
Crete, Nebraska 68333
www.dageforde.com

Printed in the United States of America
10 9 8 7 6 5 4 3 2 1

CONTENTS

This book is dedicated to my wife without whose encouragement and support it would not have been possible to write.

I am thankful to the Holy Spirit for His guidance and inspiration in the content and spiritual revelation necessary for the writing of this book.

I would also like to express my thanks to a special friend—Bob Boykin of Cary, North Carolina, for pitching in with his computer savvy. Bob's help has been a blessing for sure. His untiring time with his computer knowledge so patiently given kept me straight. Thanks Bob!

If you, the reader, have not met the Lord Jesus Christ and asked Him to come in and be a part of your life then it's time you did. He is now waiting. (John 3: 16)

For God so loved the world,
that He gave His only begotten Son,
that whosoever believeth in Him should not
perish, but have everlasting life. (KJV)

Why don't you right now bow your head and say these words as you ask Jesus into your heart and be your Savior.

Lord Jesus, I repent of my sins right now. Please for-
give me of my sins and come into my heart and save me right
now. I accept You as my Savior and my Lord. I ask and re-
ceive this in Jesus' name.

If you said this prayer I would like to hear from you so that I can send you some literature and words of encouragement to help you in your new walk.

There will be no appeals for support. I just want to be a blessing to you.

The Ol' Cowpoke
1520 Old Clayton Road
Willow Springs, NC 27592
olcowpokeone@aol.com
919 587 322

PREFACE

Although this book is fiction and written based on a desire and longing for me to have lived during the time and rigors of the Old West, the tales and experiences of the character called the Ol' Cowpoke could have happened just as they were depicted. It has been a great pleasure to take you on these few imaginary trips back into time when there were good guys and bad guys thrown together. As you will soon become aware, the good always prevails and there can be a spiritual lesson always trying to overshadow the adverse message being sent out by an ever-present evil personage called Satan. Even though the Ol' Cowpoke found himself in situations completely innocently, and in most cases not knowing what to do, he still seemed to always come out the hero.

I hope as you read and enjoy these tales that you will take the time and note the need for The Holy Spirit, as He is always present desiring to be in the lives and situations of the believer. Not only is He present but wants to become a viable part in the life of the believer as well. Thank you again for taking

the time to read and enjoy the tales of the Ol' Cow-
poke and the gang around the Delta D Ranch.

After reading the tales, if you have found a bit of
humor and pleasure in meeting the Ol' Cowpoke it
would be my pleasure to hear from you.

The Ol' Cowpoke
1520 Old Clayton Road
Willow Springs, NC 27592
olcowpokeone@aol.com

ILLUSTRATIONS

CHAPTER 1: The picture of Little Stretch was taken in the Museum of Natural History in Raleigh, North Carolina. The realism shown here speaks highly for the staff involved in the displays at the museum.

CHAPTER 2: The picture of Ol' Spirit the Wonder Horse was taken at the Berry Patch Stables in Asheville, North Carolina.

CHAPTER 3: The person posing as a rustler is Guy Keen from Raleigh, North Carolina.

CHAPTER 4: The person who filled in as Jane Ryco was none other than Rachael Mann who incidentally is the wife of the writer. Her help in the writing of *The Ol' Cowpoke Sez Howdy* will always prove how valuable she is and how much she is appreciated.

CHAPTER 5: The picture of Maude and Millie was taken on a cattle farm in Willow Springs, North Carolina.

CHAPTER 6: The Ill-Tempered Shiny One was photographed by the writer.

CHAPTER 7: The cowboy photo was taken at the Berry Patch Stables in Asheville, North Carolina. The cowboy's name is Jeff Hobbs.

CHAPTER 8: The little gold cross was loaned to the writer by Dr. Jennifer Schmidt of Apex, North Carolina.

CHAPTER 9: Jamie's kite was photographed by the writer.

CHAPTER 10: Ol' Spirit's picture was taken from a news clipping.

CHAPTER 11: The dream is Rachael Mann, the wife of the writer.

CHAPTER 12: Belle Starr is Starr Wilson of Cary, North Carolina.

CHAPTER 13: The Uncloudy Days Trio is The Dowden Sisters of Leicester, North Carolina.

CHAPTER 14: The ring hands belong to Matthew and Jackie McKinney of Cary, North Carolina.

CHAPTER 15: Rags is a colt on the Berry Patch Farm in Asheville, North Carolina.

CHAPTER 16: The village blacksmith is J.C. Knowles of Cary, North Carolina.

CHAPTER 17: Helen is Glenda Joyner of Willow Springs, North Carolina.

CHAPTER 18: Rosalie is Rosalie Brunner of Garner, North Carolina.

The varmint was photographed at the Reptile Ranch at Raleigh, North Carolina.

CHAPTER 19: The vine-covered shack is located on a cattle farm in Willow Springs, North Carolina.

The jail was photographed in a little community in Nebraska.

CHAPTER 20: The minister pictured is the writer's own pastor, Pastor Mark McKinney, and we love him very much.

CHAPTER 21: The winning smile belongs to Iris Jerkins of Raleigh, North Carolina.

CHAPTER 22: Sister Susan is Minister Susan Turcotte of Williamston, North Carolina.

The chapel was photographed at the Mordecai Historical Park in Raleigh, North Carolina.

CHAPTER 23: Annette, the farm girl, is Annette McGraw of Carthage, North Carolina.

The covered wagon is preserved on a sheep farm in Willow Springs, North Carolina.

CHAPTER 24: The couple is our pastors, Pastors Mark and Dee McKinney of Cary, North Carolina.

CHAPTER 25: The ol' vine hangs in the Museum of Natural History in Raleigh, North Carolina.

The one without his shotgun is James Sherman of Sanford, North Carolina.

CHAPTER 26: Doc Savage is the writer's own physician, Doctor Jennifer Schmidt, MD, of Apex, North Carolina.

CHAPTER 27: Carmen is Carmen Hiller of Garner, North Carolina.

CHAPTER I

The Ol' Cowpoke to the Rescue!

Are not two sparrows sold for a copper coin?
And not one of them falls to the ground apart
from your Father's will. (NKJ)
—Matthew 10:29

Well, howdy saddle pals! This here's your buddy the Ol' Cowpoke coming to sit a spell with you and spread a tall tale about the Great West. I'm just an ol' cowboy working with other ranch hands on the Delta D Ranch here near West Fork, Kansas.

Now there seems to always be something interesting happening 'round here on the Delta D. Usually it's one of the trail hands that has a story to tell but this time, I, the Ol' Cowpoke, was the lucky one to come across this tale.

It was late in the week about dusk on a very windy and dusty evening. This week had been an unusually trying one. It seemed like everything had to be done twice and took three times as long to do.

Usually after breaking camp on the trail I, the Ol' Cowpoke, want to get back to Ol' Smokey's vittles so badly that I urge Spirit, my faithful and trusty steed, into a gallop. This time, however, I just laid the reins loosely on Spirit's neck and sorta fell back in the saddle for a slow trip back to the ranch. One thing that I noticed was that for some reason my canteen had become emptier than usual and needed to be refilled pronto. I held the canteen up and examined it carefully to see if there had come a leak somewhere. I thought this was real strange because there is always enough water left for my return trip. Feeling kinda thirsty I took a side trip to where I knew an always cool and refreshing spring flowed nearby. I jumped down from Spirit and knelt down beside the spring and began to rake the leaves and sticks aside to make way for the refilling of my canteen. As I pushed my canteen under the water I noticed something sticking out of the water. What I saw really shook me up. I thought I saw a rock floating on the water. I reached to touch the thang and I coulda sworn that I saw it move. As I looked more closely I thought that I heard a breath coming from the floating rock. I reached out to touch this breathing, floating rock and to my surprise I felt it move. Upon closer observation I could see the head. Eyes were looking up at me from below the surface of the water. Understandably this was unnerving but I knew what I must do.

I went back to my horse and got a pot from my gear and my lariat from off the saddle horn and started back to the spring. I knew that if I jumped down into the water my weight would cause it to rise and come over his nose. I took my pot and bailed out a few inches of water and jumped in, boots and all. As I felt around in total darkness I could tell that it was a baby deer standing on his hind legs and reaching for all he was worth toward the life-giving air. It was all the little fellow could do just to break the surface with his nose to the air above. I took my lariat and increased the noose and slipped it down onto the fawn's middle. Having already tied the other end to the saddle horn, I began to speak gently to Spirit to begin pulling the little animal out. As I wrapped my arms around the little guy's small skeletal body I knew that this creature had been standing in this spot for over a week. I gently began lifting the fawn and as I felt the rope tighten, I could tell that Spirit could sense just how hard to pull so as not to injure the weakened body. I knew that I had to work fast before the fawn lost the battle to survive. I unrolled my blanket and wrapped it around the fawn's wet and shivering body. I then laid the animal across the saddle. I mounted Spirit and headed back to the ranch.

The ranch hands heard the hoof beats of Spirit walking across the planks of the bridge over the stream just outside the bunkhouse yard. They all ran out to meet me because I had never been this late for Ol' Smokey's Friday night steak supper. I called out for someone to bring a nursing bucket from the barn. These buckets have to be used often to feed newborn calves that the mother will not feed. Another cowhand and I took the almost lifeless fawn down from the saddle and raised his head up to where he could drink. By this time Ol' Smokey, realizing the situation, had gone to the Big House kitchen to put some milk into the bucket and was standing by. Right away the little fellow knew what to do because he took to this makeshift mother like there was no tomorrow. I stayed with the weakened fawn the rest of the night to provide warmth and additional nourishment. I did take time to eat some supper that Ol' Smokey had brought me after the excitement had quieted down.

The next morning all the ranch hands had gathered round the little deer that by now had gained enough strength to stand up on his own. They all wanted to know everything about the sustained fawn that I had rescued from certain death.

Upon hearing my recollection of the day's events, the ranch hands stood spellbound as if they had all been in on the rescue the whole time. As they all cheered, the ranch owner, Col. Dexter, from over at the Big House, heard the commotion and came to see what all the noise was about. He, too, became excited and wanted to become involved so he said, "What shall we name the little fellow?"

Upon hearing how I had found him all stretched out trying to get air he suggested, "Let's call him Stretch!"

Well, Stretch sorta fit and that's what we called our new friend.

The following Sunday, Pastor Wells had heard all about Stretch and his rescue so he included in his sermon how God's eyes are always going to and fro looking for an opportunity to show his love toward even a creature like a little deer.

He also reminded us that there were small and large animals present at the birth of Jesus the Christ Child. Pastor Wells relayed to us that he believes God through the Holy Spirit had caused my canteen to become empty and that He had sent the thirst, which made me change my direction and swing past the spring. Had He not, one of God's creatures would not have been spared. In his closing remarks, Pastor Wells encouraged and prayed that everyone would not be in such a hurry that God's voice would not be heard.

*Little **Stretch** coming right along!*

CHAPTER 2

'Round the Barn Yard with the Ol' Cowpoke and Spirit the Wonder Horse

A man that hath friends must show himself friendly, and there is a friend that sticketh closer than a brother. (KJV)
—Proverbs 18:24

Our story starts out on the afternoon just after Ol' Smokey had served us ranch hands a mighty fine supper of T-bone steak and all the trimmings.

As everyone was just sitting around chewing the rag, one of the cowhands spoke up and said, "Say CP, why have you never told us how you came about Ol' Spirit the Wonder Horse?" Well, being the shy and bashful type, I didn't usually want to bog down the cowpunchers with my tales unless I was begged.

There arose such a clatter of "Yes, yes, yes, tell us!" that I felt I had to do it. I cleared my throat, leaned back in my cane-bottomed chair, propped my feet up on the potbellied stove footrest, and began my tale.

"You see fellows, Spirit the Wonder Horse hasn't always been the most beautiful, smartest, and fastest, stallion there ever was. He started out looking like something trying to escape the glue factory bunch. Well one morning I wasn't feeling quite up to snuff so I decided to just lay around the bunkhouse and drink some of Ol' Smokey's magic elixir for our ills that's guaranteed to cure or kill you.

"About four that afternoon I decided to see if my legs would hold me up for a short walk out the back way to see if I could hear the ram rods returning from riding fence. As I walked past one of the haystacks I saw something that had not been there previously. There on the ground was a pile of rubbish. I wondered if Ol' Smokey had started another garbage dump to be buried. Upon a closer look I could tell it was a horse. I could tell this disabled creature had been trying to get to the haystack but had collapsed to the ground. I ran to the fallen horse as fast as my wobbly, weak legs would carry me.

"When I got to the poor critter I thought that it was the most beautiful animal I had ever seen, but completely uncared for and in a pitiful state. As I bent down to raise the horse's head so he could breathe without laboring, I wondered how anyone in his right mind could let this magnificent animal get in this condition. By this time the drovers had returned from fence mending and were watering their horses and getting them ready for feeding."

See, saddle pals, the most important thing a cattleman must do even before he can think of himself is to care for his horse. On a cattle drive a drover is only as good as his horse. Many times his very life may depend on the alertness of that animal he is sitting on.

"As the drovers came out of the barn they noticed Ol' Smokey rounding the corner of the bunkhouse with a bucket and some rags. They broke into a run to see where Ol' Smokey was going. All the ranch hands knew that he had an uncanny sense of need and when they saw him going toward the field they knew something was seriously wrong. Their first thought was that I had fallen or had been sicker than they thought.

"As the men got to the corner of the bunkhouse, all they could see was me leaning over a fallen horse and their knees went weak because they thought I had been thrown from my horse. The men fell in behind Ol' Smokey who had by now broken into a run toward me. The men had already started praying that I would be all right.

"After Ol' Smokey washed the sand and sweat off the horse's face and poured some water on the poor critter's dry and parched lips he noticed a remarkable change come over the animal who had just a minute before looked to be near death. It was almost like a prayer meeting to see two dozen rough cowboys just off the cattle trail kneeling around that poor horse. We all laid our hands on the horse's body and began thanking a great God for sparing this animal's life."

This was one of the things that Pastor Wells always stressed in his sermons: that no matter how things look on the surface, God our heavenly Father sees the whole picture and is always in control.

"Well, as you would expect, Col. Dexter, the ranch owner, turned the care and treating of my newfound friend over to me and day by day a marked improvement could be seen. But I had yet to find a name for him.

"Then one day as the drovers were mending some downed fences just over the rise from the ranch house, two of the ranch hands noticed me a ways off from them but they didn't see my white horse. As they approached me they asked where my friend was. I pointed to a tree about a hundred yards away and told them to watch carefully. All of a sudden a white head poked out from behind the tree and then drew back. After a few seconds it would pop out and draw back again. I told them that this had become a favorite game of my four-legged friend. One of the drovers remarked that with his white color and all, he looked like some kind of spirit. I was held aghast and told the men that I had asked the Lord to help me find a name for the white horse. He was too magnificent to just be called The White Horse, so I gave him the name Spirit."

From that day on, Spirit the Wonder Horse and I are never apart for more than a few minutes at a time.

As a matter of fact, the men accuse me of preferring Spirit's company to theirs.

Sometimes Spirit will disappear but I do not worry, he is just hiding behind his favorite tree waiting for me to come looking for him.

Pastor Well's sermon, just last Sunday, was on the subject of being faithful. He said, "No man is an island. He has to, because of his nature, belong to someone and someone has to belong to him. Jesus wants to be to us much like Spirit is to CP, our constant companion. After all, He is a friend that sticks closer than a brother."

There you have the story of how Ol' Spirit came about and how he got his name. If you should ever visit the Delta D Ranch you will probably see me, the Ol' Cowpoke, somewhere about with my faithful companion, Spirit the Wonder Horse.

*The Ol' Cowpoke and Spirit the Wonder Horse
a' looking at you!*

*This is what the Ol' Cowpoke looked like when Spirit the
Wonder Horse saw him for the first time. Scary, isn't it?*

CHAPTER 3

The Ol' Cowpoke Helps the Rustlers Accept Their Savior

He that dwells in the secret place of the most high shall abide under the shadow of the Almighty. I will say of the Lord, He is my refuge and my fortress: my God; in Him will I trust. Surely He shall deliver thee from the snare of the fowler, and from the noisome pestilence. (KJV)
—Psalms 91:1-3

Everything had been going real well during the cattle drive. Even though we had pulled a long day, everyone just seemed to want to sit and relax. I had pulled my guitar, Ol' Betsy, out of the chuck wagon and started picking a tune. This always was enjoyable to the cowboys and they all would join in and sing along. While I played and everyone was singing we didn't really notice a bunch of riders approaching the light of our campfire. The one who seemed to be the leader spoke and asked if we would share our coffee with them. I said, "Sure, hop down and grab a cup." All the riders dismounted. A dozen it turned out to be, and much to our surprise we found our-selves looking down the barrel of twelve guns of the meanest, orneriest men I had ever seen. Needless to say, we were completely in shock.

The leader said, "Okay, boys, we have come to take these cows off your hands."

I couldn't believe what happened next! I, the Ol' Cowpoke, who usually is the shy and bashful type, jumped up and shouted to these cattle rustlers, "Oh no you don't, they belong to Lord Jehovah, and He owns the cattle on a thousand hills and He owns the hills too and you better watch it buster!" I was absolutely stunned at my boldness and figured my time had come.

The leader leaned back, laughed, and said, "Who is this Lord Jehovah? Is he someone from England who has just come over here and bought a spread? He must be real new because I know all the cattle owners for miles around! Heh, heh."

I said, "You don't understand, but Lord Jehovah is the great God Almighty and He has legions of angels protecting His property and that includes us cowboys. You see sir, we have accepted God's son Jesus as our Savior and now everything we have belongs to Him."

"Tell me ramrod," the leader questioned, "how can I accept Jesus and have Him as my Savior?"

I said, "Sir, all you have to do is ask Jesus to come into your heart, forgive your sins, and you become as clean as new fallen snow."

Suddenly the man bowed his head and said, "Jesus, I'm sorry for the way I have been doing. Will You come into my heart and be my Savior?"

The man turned to the other rustlers and said, "You fellows go on without me because I'm going with these cowboys."

They all replied, "Oh no you don't, we want to have a Savior too!"

To my surprise, the other eleven bowed their heads and asked Jesus to come into their hearts.

When we got back to the Delta D Ranch we told Col. Dexter what had happened. Would you believe he hired the whole dozen? You can figure we had a camp meeting that night. And you can believe I pranced around like a rooster for the next couple of days because to everyone around the ranch I was considered a real hero.

Well as you have already guessed, Pastor Wells had prepared his sermon so that he could preach a little about the protection of God's children and how He keeps them from harm.

Pastor Wells said it was the protection of our friends in the time of danger. Would you believe that Pastor Wells received all twelve of these former rustlers? He put them under the watch care of the church until such time as they had been instructed in the ways of the church. He made sure they knew what it was to serve the Lord Jesus Christ with all their heart and they were then invited to join West Fork church and were baptized.

Don't move. We want all your cattle and your wagon, too.

From rustler to fisherman for Jesus.

CHAPTER 4

Jane Ryco, the World's Greatest Sharpshooter, Comes to Visit

And do not be called leaders; for one is your leader, that is, Christ. But the greatest among you shall be your servant. And whoever exalts himself shall be humbled; and whoever humbles himself shall be exalted. (NASV)
—Matthew 23:10-12

Boy, the ol' ranch has never been a buzz with excitement like it's been these last few days! Ever since the cat was let out of the bag about a long-time famous friend of mine coming to the ranch. Matter of fact, I was a pure hero for miles around. Ol' Smokey even promised me a double portion of apple pie for a whole month if I would arrange for Jane to sit with him just one time at the dining table. (I just love apple pie!) I told him I would see what I could do.

Soon each cowboy had a similar request, each promising to give me a prized possession. They offered everything from a knife to a saddle for the honor of Jane's presence next to them.

You should have seen the brooms a flying and the dust swirling around so heavy that you couldn't tell what had been swept and what had not!

Finally the day arrived that Jane was to come in on the three o'clock train to the big city of West Fork. Every ranch hand had bathed and had been to the barbershop to have their beard trimmed and hair slicked down. When they walked down the street, the scent of bay rum was so overpowering that the passersby were almost lifted off the ground.

It was a sight to behold seeing two dozen rugged cowhands acting like kids who just went to town for the first time. At the station they were all standing in a single line and each one begging the train to stop where he was so that Jane would step down right in front of him. I thought I was going to get whipped when Jane ran and threw her arms around my neck. No one was really mad at me because they knew Jane and I were the best of friends.

For the next few days the ranch was so neat it shined, so Col. Dexter considered hiring Jane just to hang around. Her presence alone was lifting spirits and making everyone work their hardest to impress her.

The men had all pitched in and cleared a piece of land. They also made a firing range complete with seats and everything.

The long awaited day was here for Jane's performance and all the cowboys were scrambling for the best seat.

I went into the barn and saddled up Spirit the Wonder Horse. This was the first time that Jane had seen Spirit and it was love at first sight for the two of them. Spirit took to Jane right off just like the men did. He was on his best behavior and did a few fancy prances to show off for her.

Jane jumped in the saddle and started for the firing range. As she drew near, the ground shook and there was a yell of excitement that could be heard for miles. Ol' Smokey was left to stand guard and let everyone know when Jane was near. To my surprise the men had put up a banner stretching all the way from the bunkhouse to the firing range. On this banner they had painted the words "Welcome to Jane Ryco The Greatest!" The banner would be a reminder of Jane's visit because the men had taken the plant bed cover off the new tomato plants and Ol' Smokey would make sure that it was put back.

As Jane rode in everyone noticed that she was carrying a feed sack nailed to a cross. As Jane came within sight between the two rows of chairs, we noticed a picture on the cloth she was carrying. The place was in complete silence. As one of the men wiped a tear from his eye, we heard him whisper, "It's Jesus, it's Jesus."

When Jane raised her hand there was absolute silence and she began to speak. "No, precious ones, I am not the Greatest." Jane held up the cloth as high as she could reach and shouted to the top of her voice, "He is!"

At that, the place came alive with ear shattering hooting and hollering.

Jane had met Pastor Wells the day before and she called upon him to pray and ask God to use her talents to glorify His name and to bring praise and honor to Jesus that He would be lifted up even in an event like a display of sharp shooting.

For the next two hours Jane put on a show like no one had ever seen before. There was trick riding, roping, and shooting. It was evident that Jane was indeed the greatest performer in the world.

It was unbelievable how Spirit followed every command Jane whispered to him. It seemed he could sense every move even before she spoke. I had tears in my eyes as I witnessed this trust between a beautiful lady and a great horse.

A special room had been prepared in the Big House for Jane, but she didn't get to stay in it very much because her every need was tended to by two dozen ranch hands who will never forget the time Jane Ryco came to visit.

In Pastor Well's sermon Sunday, he complimented the men for making this time special for Jane and for letting her feel a part of each one of them.

Jane had called Pastor Wells aside and told him that the few days spent with them at the Delta D Ranch showed her just a little bit of heaven and what it will be like to be there.

As the train was pulling away from the station, all the men once again gathered in a single line and leaned out as far as they could toward Jane. They could hear her uplifting words, "If I don't see you here, I'll see you there or in the air. God bless you. You will remain constantly in my prayers forever. I love you."

Those were the last words they heard Jane say as the train rattled down the track, around the bend, and out of sight.

All my companions and I stood motionless for a time. Without a word, we mounted our horses and started the trip back to the ranch. As we rode away we each gave a last wave toward the train that had disappeared from sight. As swift as she came, she left, and Jane became just a memory that would never be

 forgotten by two dozen rugged cowboys who felt they had been in the presence of an angel.

Jane Ryco.
The World's Greatest Sharpshooter.

*The West Fork Depot right
after Jane had pulled away.*

CHAPTER 5

'Round the Barnyard with the Ol' Cowpoke and his Newfound Friends, Maude and Millie

As Jesus approached Jerusalem,
and was near the town of Bethphage on the
Mount of Olives, Jesus sent two
of them into the village ahead.
"Just as you enter," He said, "you will see a
donkey tied there, with its colt beside it. Untie
them and bring them here. If anyone asks you
what you are doing, just say, "The master needs
them," and there will be no trouble.
This was done to fulfill the ancient prophecy,
"Tell Jerusalem her King is coming to her,
riding humbly on a donkey's colt!" (LB)
—Matthew 21:1-4

Howdy saddle pals! Ready for another great story about the Old West? Here's one ya might like.

We ranch hands were out on a cattle drive one day, except Ol' Smokey, who had a bout with the flu and had to stay behind. But as soon as he got his strength up, Ol' Smokey went over to West Fork and had lunch with Pastor Wells at the Diamond T restaurant. While they were eating, Bennie, the owner came over to their table and asked if he could sit with them a spell. They asked him what he had on his mind as he joined them at their table.

"My brother Blake just arrived from back east and is looking for a job," Bennie explained. "He used to be a cook for a halfway house but wanted to come out to Kansas to see what the other end of the world was like. Now Blake's a serious camper and is used to cooking and eating in the outdoors. He usually takes his vacation time to go out in the rugged mountain ranges of North and South Carolina to camp. He backpacks to wherever he can find a spot to his liking and stays there for the entire time. In fact, he's always trying to find a camping spot that's more rugged and demanding than the last."

"Well, just the other day Col. Dexter mentioned to me that there was a possible opening for a trail cook on the ranch," Ol' Smokey explained. "Anyone being considered for hirin' has to meet all the ranch hands first, so you should have Blake come out to the ranch to sit down and talk with us about this job opportunity."

"Great! In fact, I'll personally accompany Blake out to the ranch to get together with the ranch hands!"

Ol' Smokey explained how we were out on a cattle drive but that he'd take Blake out to meet us since we were nearly back to the ranch by now.

Ol' Smokey, Bennie, and Blake jumped into their saddles and headed to meet up with the trail herd. They reached us about dusk. Ol' Smokey told me they were there for us to meet Blake, so I suggested we camp there for the night to give Blake a chance to meet the cowboys and get a feel first-hand what it was like on a cattle drive.

Ol' Smokey usually does the cooking, but since he was not able to come on this cattle drive, the cooking had become part of my job.

Just like he did the chuck wagon, Blake took to the cooking. We could tell that he was no stranger to this kind of life and would really fit in. He grabbed pots and pans and whatever food he could find and began throwing together a meal fit for a king. I believe Ol' Smokey himself was quite impressed.

After supper we all gathered around the campfire and started sharing stories about the cattle drive. All of a sudden we heard a sound and Ol' Smokey, Bennie, and Blake jumped from their seats. It sounded like an animal out of breath. The "hee haw, hee haw, hee haw" sound could be heard for miles.

Ol' Smokey asked, "What in the Sam Hill is that sound?"

I laughed and told him that it was our newfound friends, Maude and her foal Millie, who had traveled with us for the last thirty miles or so. I began to tell the three of them the story of how the burro and her foal had become a part of our drive.

"About thirty miles away we came upon a camp. Tied to a small tree was this burro lying on her side with a rope all twisted around her neck restricting her airflow. I started to loosen the rope to let her breathe when low and behold a voice that seemed to come from nowhere bellowed out, 'What are you doing with my mule? Who gave you permission to untie her? I have a good mind to shoot the whole lot of you.'

"He looked like he could do it too because he raised the longest shotgun I have ever seen and pointed it straight at us!

"I said, 'Wait a minute, we were just trying to help her get her breath. We were not trying to steal her or anything.'

"We noticed that there were marks on her body that led us to believe she had been beaten so badly that she could not even stand up. I said that he could shoot if he wanted to but I was going to untie her and put some salve on her wounds.

"I went to the chuck wagon where Ol' Smokey always keeps handy a good supply of medicine for the many scrapes and scratches that are normal on a cattle drive.

"After helping the burro, we looked over a ways. There was her foal. It looked like it had not been allowed to feed since she was born.

"I asked the fellow how he could treat animals like this and he told me to butt out and that it was none of my business. Then I asked the fellow if he would sell the burro and her foal to me and I asked what he wanted for them. The fellow told me that he didn't have any use for those sorry pieces of flesh and that I could have them for fifty dollars. I didn't have but five dollars but among the ramrods we managed to put together forty-nine dollars and thirty-nine cents.

"I handed the fellow what money I had and he jerked it out of my hand so hard that the change fell to the ground. The fellow just walked off mumbling to himself something about someone always trying to take advantage of him and his good nature.

"I followed after the fellow trying to tell him that Jesus loved him and wouldn't he consider letting Him into his heart to be his Savior. The fellow, we never did learn his name, was not interested in the least but I had planted a seed and now it was up to the Holy Spirit to do the growing.

"We stayed an additional day there while we tended to the burro's wounds. We had to hold her up so the foal could nurse. By the day after, the burro had regained much of her strength and we were able to get the herd moving again."

By the time I finished telling the story of Maude and Millie, everyone was ready to hit the bedroll.

The next morning we woke mighty early to the aroma of coffee, bacon, and other good smells that really made us all realize how we had missed Ol' Smokey and his vittles while he was out sick. But Blake had already gotten up and had prepared a delicious breakfast and we knew right away that we wanted him for out trail cook, if and when we ever needed one.

We broke camp and our newfound friends, Maude and Millie were placed in the chuck wagon all wrapped up warm as could be. By the time we reached the ranch, Blake was considered one of the bunch, and for the time being Blake was given the position of assistant to Ol' Smokey, and is working out just fine.

How it happens is still somewhat of a mystery to me, but Pastor Wells always hits right on target a message that is sometimes scary because of its accuracy. Matter of fact, his sermon Sunday was based on the Scripture from St. Matthew's Gospel.

If any of ya'll saddle pals are ever at the Delta D and you hear a blood curdling sound like I described a time back and you look around you will probably see our ol' buddies Maude and Millie. Incidentally, they are pretty grown up by now. Maude and Millie are doin' just fine.

W. Odell Mann

We got Millie's attention!

CHAPTER 6

The Ol' Cowpoke Meets Doc Percy in a Stinging Way

For verily I say unto you, that whosoever shall say unto this mountain, be thou removed, and be cast into the sea; and shall not doubt in his heart, but shall believe that those things which he saith shall come to pass; he shall have whatsoever he saith. Therefore I say unto you, what things so ever ye desire, when ye pray, believe that ye receive them, and ye shall have them. (KJV)
—Mark 11:23-24

Howdy saddle pals! Into each life some rain must fall, even in one like mine, the Ol' Cowpoke's, who can withstand almost anything. It all started one morning right after we had come back from one of the most backbreaking roundups that I had ever been on before. All the ranch hands had gathered at the breakfast table of Ol' Smokey's famous eggs and pork chops, when someone questioned, "Where is CP?" At that, Ol' Smokey's ears perked up because he knew that it was not like me to be late for breakfast. In fact, no one had better get in my way going to the table. Ol' Smokey himself had to check out why I was not at my regular place. Right behind Ol' Smokey, twenty-two anxious rough rowdies started toward the bunkhouse.

Ol' Smokey opened the door and called out, "CP?"

There was no answer so he went on in with twenty-two cowboys right behind. Ol' Smokey called out again, "CP, you in here?"

Ol' Smokey became nervous when he noticed that the windows were covered over and there was no sunlight coming through. I could never stand darkness in the bunkhouse during the daylight hours and the guys knew this.

Ol' Smokey was now getting mighty upset and felt his way to the window to raise the shade. Then he went straight to my bunk and discovered that I was all covered up head to toe. Ol' Smokey turned the covers down a little and could tell that I was shaking. He reached out and laid his hand on my forehead and realized that I was burning up. Ol' Smokey is quite the medic, always having to tend to scratches and scrapes on the trail. This time Ol' Smokey knew he was out of his league and needed to call upon a professional.

He turned and headed for the Big House. Sensing trouble, Col. Dexter met Ol' Smokey at the door. (Nothing ever interrupts breakfast or there will be trouble with a capital T.) Ol' Smokey told Col. Dexter what he knew. Col. Dexter became alarmed.

They hurried over to my bunk, and as Col. Dexter walked in, Dusty, one of the cowhands standing beside my bunk blurted out that I was motionless. When Col. Dexter pulled the cover back from over my face he commanded Ol' Smokey to have Nancy phone Doc Percy to tell him that Col. Dexter wanted him to come as quickly as possible.

As soon as Nancy called, Doc Percy grabbed his bag and as he went out the door yelled to Frances, his nurse, to tell all his patients that he had an emergency and had to leave immediately.

After Doc Percy had gone, Frances went back to the phone and told Nancy that Doc Percy was on his way and that she would stand by the phone in case she was needed.

It wasn't very long before Doc Percy came busting through the bunkhouse door. He didn't even take time to introduce himself to everyone who hadn't met him. He just ran to my bedside and as soon as he saw me, said to call Silver City Hospital and tell them to prepare an anti-venom shot because he was bringing in a patient from the Delta D Ranch.

Doc Percy insisted that Frances call Pastor Wells and tell him to gather the whole church and get them praying. Doc Percy said that if the Lord did not intervene, I would not have made it to the hospital in time.

Pastor Wells wasted no time in gathering the prayer warriors and intercession was started for my healing. Prayer continued the rest of the day and on into the night.

About five o' clock the next morning the telephone rang and Frances picked it up before it finished its first ring. Doc Percy said that prayer had worked! My breathing had returned to normal and my color was returning.

Frances, without hesitation shouted out, "Praise God forever!"

Doc Percy said that he would be staying to monitor me the rest of the night and for her to call Col. Dexter and let everyone know that I was on the mend and to thank them for their prayers. It was learned the next day that a black widow spider had bitten me and had remained in my clothing. The specialist at the hospital told Doc Percy that if it had been ten more minutes there would have been no need to bring me in.

As Doc Percy was returning to West Fork the next day he noticed that it took him two and a half hours for the return trip. He calculated that the total time that elapsed the night before was only forty-five minutes. The good Lord had been with us to guide our swift journey.

Sunday morning, Pastor Wells' whole sermon was geared around the goodness of God and how He always is in the business of doing the impossible.

Pastor Wells told the congregation that he was proud to report that I was feeling much better and that I send my love and thanks for their prayers and that I miss worshiping there with them.

Doc Percy had only been in West Fork for one day when all this happened. The mayor had been seeking a new physician for almost a year. Ain't God good? Praise His holy name!

The Ill-Tempered Shiny One.

CHAPTER 7

The Ol' Cowpoke Meets Sparks McKinney, Bronc Buster

*But a certain Samaritan, as he journeyed, came where was:
and when he saw him, he had compassion on him.
And went to him, and bound up his wounds,
pouring in oil and wine, and set him on his own beast, and
brought him to an inn, and took care of him.
And on the morrow when he departed, he took out two
pence, and gave them to the host, and said unto him,
"Take care of him; and whatsoever thou spendest more,
when I come again, I will repay thee." (KJV)*
—Luke 10:33-35

The Lord just keeps on blessing and blessing the Delta D Ranch. As a matter of fact, when the semi-annual roundup was over, low and behold the herd had increased by fifteen hundred head. Everyone kept asking how this could happen. The only answer that we could come up with was as the Bible says, God owns the cattle on a thousand hills and He wanted to give us some. Right now there is only one horse for each cowhand. Col. Dexter, the ranch owner, recognized that this was not sufficient, so he went to a big stock sale over in the neighboring county and came back with twelve great looking quarter horses. The only problem was that no one had the time to break the new horses before the next roundup. As always the Lord came through in a great and mighty way.

All of us cowhands had just sat down to a supper of Ol' Smokey's world famous T-Bone steak, mashed potatoes, and fresh vegetables right from the garden. Ol' Smokey always had a giant garden because as he put it, "I want to see where my vittles come from."

As we were just finishing blessing the food and were starting to eat, there was a knock on the mess hall door. Everyone looked at each other with bewilderment as to who would have wandered this far from the well-traveled road. It seemed like a long time before anyone made an effort to go to the door. Finally Will Baxter, who was sitting the closest to the door, went and opened it. Everyone's eyes fell on the fellow standing outside. There was a shabbily dressed young man probably in his mid-twenties looking half-starved staring back at them. Ol' Smokey went to the kitchen and brought out a plate piled up with everything he could find to eat. The young man was invited to wash up and sit down at the head of the table. This place had always been left vacant as a special invitation for the Holy Spirit to sit. Tonight everyone seemed to agree that it was appropriate to sit our visiting stranger at this place. The stranger, after gobbling down most of his food, started to tell us his story and how he came to be at our out-of-the-way door.

"I'm Sparks McKinney, on my way to a small, unheard of town. My Model T knocked off a while back so I just started walking. By this time darkness had settled in and just as I came over the hill there before my unbelieving eyes was the light shining through your windows! I was almost to the point of exhaustion but I stepped up my pace as much as I could toward your mess hall."

"What's your occupation, Sparks?" I asked.

"I'm a bronc buster at a quarter horse ranch over in the next state. I just got word that my father up north is very ill so I'm trying to get there before he passes away."

The whole bunch of us could not believe what we were hearing! We knew the good Lord guided Sparks to us.

After supper Ol' Smokey took Sparks over to the ranch house and introduced him to Col. Dexter. He told him Sparks' story and Col. Dexter told Ol' Smokey to fix up one of the guest rooms for our visitor. He also said that the next morning after breakfast we were to hitch up the buckboard and I was to take Sparks to meet the train for the trip up north. It so happens there was some clothes that were hanging in the closet that just fit Sparks and early in the morning after he had bathed and cleaned up, we started for the train station.

As Sparks was bidding me so long, I passed into his hand an envelope with enough money for his trip up north and back to the Delta D Ranch if he chose to do so. Those were the instructions from Col. Dexter. I told Sparks that if he chose to return all he had to do was ask anyone at the train station to drive him to the Delta D and they would be happy to do so.

As the train was rattling off, I whispered a prayer of thanksgiving to my heavenly Father for sending Sparks McKinney to our front door and allowing us, a bunch of lowly cowpunchers, to show kindness to someone in need. I asked that He also watch over Sparks and provide him safe travel.

In his sermon Sunday, Pastor Wells, after hearing the story of Sparks' visit, remarked that our experience was much like the Good Samaritan. He felt that Sparks was divinely guided to our ranch and that he would return much like he came.

Sparks has not accepted Jesus as his Savior yet but I believe God is not through with him and that He has great work for him to do.

Hang in there Sparks! Show him who's boss!

CHAPTER 8

The Copper-Haired Boy
and the Little Gold Cross

*Continue to love each other with true brotherly love.
Don't forget to be kind to strangers, for some
who have done this have entertained angels
without realizing it! (LB)*
—Hebrews 13 :1-2

One of the most interesting occasions that has ever happened to me was on the last roundup when we all decided to go to town after we had bedded down the cattle for the night. That is, all except for four rowdies that we left to watch the herd. I, the Ol' Cowpoke needed some shaving cream and other articles that were running short back at the bunkhouse. I found a little store that had about everything you could imagine.

As I walked into the store I couldn't help but notice a small gold cross statue standing in the display window. Close by the little statue was a card that read seven dollars and thirty-nine cents, including tax. A quaint, stately-looking gentleman was also looking at it.

I don't know why I happened to notice the little cross statue but the man behind the counter saw our interest and walked over to us.

"A small copper-haired boy with thick freckles comes into the store daily to take a gander at that gold statue," the clerk explained. "He sits down on the wooden porch out there and pours out a small paper sack of coins that he always carries. He's got a bunch of pennies, some nickels, a few dimes, and couple of quarters. Then he counts them out one by one.

"Now when the little boy left yesterday he had a grin on his face. I think he just might be near to having enough to make his desired purchase."

The clerk smiled and returned behind the counter.

As the gentleman and I looked out the window we saw the little lad coming up the street. He wore the same grin on his face that he had the day before according to the clerk behind the counter. We could see a spring in the little boy's step and he didn't stop on the porch this time but came straight in and proudly approached the counter.

Barely able to reach the top of the counter, he emptied his little sack of coins in a small pile. There were a bunch of pennies, some nickels, a few dimes, and several quarters, just as the clerk had explained.

The ecstatic little lad politely said, "Mister, I've come to buy my little gold cross in the window."

The clerk counted the heap of coins lying on the counter. When he had finished counting he looked down at the little copper-haired boy who was standing gazing at him with a look of determination. Nothing could have prepared the lad for the statement that came next from the fellow behind the counter.

"Son, you only have seven dollars and thirty-nine cents here," he explained. "The price for the little gold cross is nine dollars and forty-nine cents."

The little lad could not contain himself and began to cry. The price tag he had read was for the pocketknife lying close by.

The young boy proclaimed, "You don't understand, Mister, how long I've been saving up to buy that cross in the window. I've been selling bottles, taking out trash, and picking up paper on yards for the owners, just to buy my cross." The lad stood completely heartbroken.

The up-town gentleman standing next to me asked the boy, "Why would you want something that is not telling the truth? I thought that Jesus was crucified on an old rugged, rough, and ugly old cross, not a shiny gold, very pretty one."

"Yes," the little lad replied as he wiped the tears from his eyes, "but Mister, don't you realize that anything Jesus touches cannot stay ugly?"

The gentleman was uplifted and impressed by the wisdom of such a small boy that he reached into his pocket and pulled out two crisp one-dollar bills and laid them on the stack of coins. He then reached into his pocket and came out with a dime and placed it on the dollar bills.

The clerk leaned over the counter and with a grin said, "Son, the cross is all yours."

The little lad ran to the window, reached in, and excitedly brought out the little shiny cross statue and tucked it into the bib of his overalls.

Just as he reached the door he stopped, turned around and hollered back, "Thanks, Mister!" He turned and ran down the street and disappeared.

I have to admit as I stood there I, too, had a lump in my throat and a sparkle in my eye that could have been mistaken for a tear. I turned to thank the gentleman for his generosity but almost fell over when he was nowhere to be seen.

"Hmm…he must have gone out the back door," I suggested.

"There is no back door," the clerk explained.

We never knew who the gentleman was nor where he came from.

I heard Pastor Wells say in his sermon the following Sunday that sometimes we are in the presence of angels. We never know when the ever-loving heavenly Father may send a special messenger to bring joy to someone.

One thing is certain, that this old rugged cowpuncher will never be the same and will always be looking over his shoulder just waiting for his special visitor.

The little gold cross that shined after Jesus' touch.

CHAPTER 9

'Round the Campfire with the Ol' Cowpoke and his Friends

But what does it say? "The Word is near you, in your mouth and in your heart" that is, the word of faith which we are preaching, that if you confess with your mouth Jesus as Lord, and believe in your heart that God raised Him from the dead, you shall be saved; for with the heart man believes, resulting in righteousness, and with the mouth he confesses, resulting in salvation. For the Scripture says, "whoever believes in Him will not be disappointed." (LB)
—Romans 10:8-11

Howdy saddle pals and a great day to you one and all! Well, here we are again 'round the ol' chuck wagon. It seems that the best times we have on the trail happen at meal time. The way my backside feels I can tell I must have spent quite a spell in the saddle today. Mr. Tucker, the trail boss, said we goofed off too much yesterday and that Col. Dexter wouldn't like our not getting the herd to the ranch and ready for market tomorrow. He was referring to the time we spent jawing with our minister Pastor Wells and his son Jamie the previous day.

Yesterday, before we all got to where Ol' Smokey had stopped the chuck wagon, we could see that there was someone with him. I, being the curious type, rode on ahead to see who Ol' Smokey's guest was because we were still quite a ways from the ranch. When I rode up I noticed that it was Pastor Wells and his son Jamie who was holding a ball of twine. I asked Jamie what he was doing and he politely replied, "Why, Mr. Cowpoke, I'm flying a kite."

By this time Mr. Tucker had ridden up and heard what Jamie said. He said to Jamie, "I don't see a kite, Jamie. How do you know it's up there?"

Jamie excitedly replied, "I feel the tug on the string."

Pastor Wells jumped up from where he was sitting with such vigor that he turned the coffee pot over in the fire. Pastor Wells without any notice about the coffee pot bellowed out, "That's just like the Holy Spirit! We can't see Him, but we know He's there because we can feel the gentle tug on our heart strings!"

With that we had an old time prayer meeting right there on the cattle trail. Pastor Wells never misses a chance to preach a little. We always enjoy his coming around because he always has a great message for us.

We had prayed a long time for God to send Pastor Wells to us and we have quickly fallen in love with the Wells' family, including his wife Rachel, and their son Jamie. It's amazing how the Holy Spirit will give Pastor Wells a sermon from daily activities around here. Matter of fact, in his Sunday sermon Pastor Wells referred to the situation of the kite and tug on the string.

Can you feel the tug?

Lo and behold, it's Jamie's kite-eating tree!

CHAPTER 10

The Ol' Cowpoke's Encounter with the Smokehouse Bear

*About four o'clock in the morning Jesus came
to them, walking on the water! They screamed
in terror, for they thought He was a ghost. But
Jesus immediately spoke to them. Reassuring
them. "Don't be afraid!" He said. (LB)*
—Matthew 14:25-27

There seems to never be a dull moment 'round the
Delta D, even when we all try to lay back and soak up
a little relaxation. Why just the other day after a real
heavy day on the range, Col. Dexter told all of us
ranch hands that we could have a day of doing just
what we wanted to do. Everyone wanted to just nap
the whole day long.

About noon, Ol' Smokey came running into the
bunkhouse screaming that some kind of a beast with
shiny eyes was in the smokehouse and it was after
him. The smokehouse is so pitch dark that even in
broad daylight you can't see your hand in front of
you. Ol' Smokey said the eyes were so bright that he

could see them in the dark. He said the thing was shaped like it had an appetite for a fat cook!

Everyone was awake by now so we each grabbed a big stick and headed for a heroic rescue for our pal Ol' Smokey. I grabbed a lantern from the wall and lit it on the run. Since I was the one with the lantern you know who was let in first. I really didn't believe there was a bear in the smokehouse anyway.

I opened the door and reached in as far as I could to see what had frightened Ol' Smokey so badly. The door slammed behind me. All of a sudden in the light I saw it. There across the room was sure 'nuff a pair of fierce looking eyes staring back at me. I wanted to turn and run but my legs were solid as stone. I even tried to yell but I had no voice. I thought my time had come and I was the bear's lunch.

Just about then the door opened. There stood the other cowboys laughing so hard that they all fell to the ground. There, standing over against the back wall licking the salt that Ol' Smokey used to preserve meat, was none other than Spirit the Wonder Horse. No one knows how he got in the smokehouse. If horses could talk it would be quite a story of twelve rugged cowpunchers so scared that we were shaking in our boots. When I finally regained my voice I called out to Spirit. He turned and walked toward me and rubbed his nose against my cheek as if to say, "What are you nuts laughing at?"

Sunday morning during pastor Wells' sermon, he of course had to give his two cents worth about our seeing a bear shaped like a horse. He talked about one occasion Jesus appeared to His disciples and they thought that He was a ghost. The disciples were so frightened that their knees knocked together and would not move! I guess Jesus probably was like Spirit wondering where all these nuts came from!

Spirit, the bear shaped like a horse.
Or is it a horse shaped like a bear?

CHAPTER 11

The Ol' Cowpoke Gets Hitched!

The man who finds a wife finds a good thing:
she is a blessing to him from the Lord. (LB)
—Proverbs 18:22

Well howdy again saddle pals! This time you caught me standing in front of the giant fireplace in the Big House. This is the place where Col. Dexter, the ranch owner, lives. Also, this is where all the decisions for the operation of the ranch are made. Another one was made here just the other day when we came off the cattle trail and had brought back probably the biggest herd that we had ever rounded up at one time. This was the first time that all two dozen cowhands had been on a roundup together. Most of the time Col. Dexter sends only a third of the cowboys on a roundup. This time, however, there was mention that it looked like a twister might be heading our way and the cattle sure didn't need to be out on the range if this happened.

Ol' Smokey was getting pretty low on vittles on the chuck wagon, so he left the drive a few miles out and went on to the ranch to restock.

When Ol' Smokey drove back into camp after restocking, we could tell by the look on his face that something had happened. We tried to get him to tell us what he was looking so sheepish about. Well Ol' Smokey can never keep a secret, so he blurted out that Col. Dexter wanted to see me, the Ol' Cowpoke, bathed and presentable in the Big House right now. (When Col. Dexter says right now, we know he means right now.)

I couldn't imagine what this was all about. No one told Ol' Smokey what it was because everyone knew he would not be able to keep from telling us.

I hurried and saddled up Spirit the Wonder Horse and lit out in full gallop toward the ranch. As soon as I got there none other than Col. Dexter himself met me at the hitching rail just outside of the bunkhouse. Col. Dexter told me to go straight to the shower and make myself presentable. We had taken a stall back in one corner of the barn and built ourselves a shower complete with hot and cold running water.

After I had unsaddled and put Spirit in his stall, I gave him some grain and his prized lump of sugar. Then I headed for the bunkhouse for some clean clothes and to shower.

Since I didn't have the slightest idea why I was wanted in the Big House, naturally I was getting a little concerned.

Pretty soon I was all clean and polished and headed for the unknown. At the door I was met by Nancy. Col. Dexter had put her in charge of the operation of the Big House. She led me to the meeting room and told me to stand by the fireplace and close my eyes because I had a surprise coming. Well, like a sheep being led to slaughter I obeyed, although I could not stand the suspense. Even though it could not have been more than a few seconds, it seemed like an hour before Nancy told me to open my eyes. When I opened them I could not believe what I saw right there in front of me. Or better, who I saw standing before my very eyes. I didn't think anything could ever be more beautiful than Spirit but this beauty surpassed all. There stood the woman that had consumed my thoughts for months. Right in front of me stood none other than Jane Ryco.

At first I thought I was dreaming and I would soon awake to find myself staring at a dumb old cow. I felt my heart in my throat as I peered at the beauty that had occupied my daydreams while on the cattle drive. When she had left the ranch after her last visit I began to regularly write to her every chance I got. As we corresponded I could tell that I was becoming fonder and fonder of Jane. As a matter of fact, I got so anxious that I couldn't bear to wait for her letters to arrive. The letter writing became more frequent and we discovered that there was more to our affection toward each other than we thought possible. I got to the place that I had her on my mind day and night. Even Col. Dexter noticed that I was moping around like a sick calf, as he put it. Without anyone knowing about it, Jane and I had started making plans for me to catch the train to come see her. Actually, I was to leave right after we finished our roundup. The last few miles of the cattle trail became so nerve racking for me that Ol' Smokey was about to send me on ahead to get me out of the cowhands' hair.

When Ol' Smokey told me that Col. Dexter wanted to see me right then I thought it had something to do with my lousy attitude. Then when Col. Dexter told me I was to clean up before coming into the Big House I thought that he had invited a neighboring ranch owner to come over and meet me because I might be needing a job. My mind was playing tricks on me and I was imagining every possible scenario.

When I finally realized that it truly was Jane I almost tripped over my own feet and fell over her. We jumped into one another's arms and there was no question about how we felt. Col. Dexter somehow had found out about my plans to meet Jane so he sent her a telegram asking her to be a surprise guest at the ranch.

Jane moved into the Big House and we spent every possible moment together. We began to speak of marriage and plans for a December wedding began to take shape. We chose a winter wedding because things are slowest around the ranch at this time. The plans intensified as the wedding date drew near. Jane and Nancy did most of the planning as there was still a never-ending parade of work that I had to do around the ranch even in winter.

Finally the big day arrived and the Big House looked like a wedding chapel with all the hanging banners and streamers. Everyone was dressed in his or her finest, including Pastor Wells in his black suit and Mrs. Wells in her bright yellow dress accessorized with a wide brim hat with big, artificial flowers.

Jane wanted to be married in the ranch house with only those on the ranch attending. Nancy was from the old school and she insisted I not see the bride before the wedding.

As I took my place before the fireplace along with Pastor Wells; Ol' Smokey, my best man; and the matron of honor, Nancy. Nancy's tears were already flowing. We didn't have a piano on the ranch so Dusty, one of the cowboys, started playing "Here Comes The Bride" on the guitar. The sounds from the old, out-of-tune guitar and of a bawling bridesmaid filled the rafters. Jane proceeded down the aisle in her stunning white wedding dress. My knees began knocking so loudly, adding to the sound of the out-of-tune guitar and the bawling bridesmaid that provided the background for our nuptials. None other than Col. Dexter was escorting Jane down the aisle and he, too, was quite the showoff.

As Pastor Wells started the wedding ceremony the door to the room burst open and in shoved what looked like the whole town of West Fork.

The mayor was the first one in and bellowed out, "We have come to see CP get hisself hitched!"

Cowboys and townsfolk spilled out the door and just about filled the front yard. Pastor Wells, however, didn't miss a word throughout the disruptions. He closed with a prayer and pronounced us man and wife. Everyone stood and cheered and threw their hats into the air. As Jane and I went out the door, all the people from town cascaded us with pounds of rice.

Col. Dexter hitched up the buckboard and then handed us two round trip tickets to Fort Worth, Texas, for a two-week honeymoon. He jokingly added that if we came back a day early, I was fired.

When Jane and I boarded the train for Fort Worth, the whole bunch from the ranch had arrived and began waving and cheering as the train rattled off and disappeared around the bend.

Ol' Smokey told me after we returned that he had overheard Pastor Wells say as the train pulled out, "There goes a happy man!"

Well, saddle pals, Pastor Wells was right I—was and still am a happy man. My life took on new meaning that day. Incidentally as Pastor Wells was shaking my hand just prior to boarding the train he slipped into my hand the words from Proverbs 18:22:

The man who finds a wife finds a good thing;
she is a blessing to him from the Lord. (LB)

Ain't she a dream?

CP just don't know what's
happening next!

CHAPTER 12

The Ol' Cowpoke Helps Establish Belle Starr's Hat and Dress Shop

*If my people which are called by my Name will
humble themselves and pray and seek my face
and turn from their wicked ways, then I will
hear from Heaven, forgive their sins, and heal
their land. (LB)*
—II Chronicles 7:14

Just when I thought I had met all the great and interesting people newly arriving to West Fork there always comes another. Saddle pals, let me introduce to you our hat and dress store owner Miss Jessica (Belle) Starr. The first time I met Belle I knew she was the most delightful person I had ever met, next to Jane Ryco of course.

My new wife, Jane, and I were returning from our honeymoon in Fort Worth. As we stepped off the train, we noticed a very classy, uptown looking lady who was also exiting the train at West Fork. Jane and I introduced ourselves to this lady. We learned that she was Jessica Starr from Amarillo and that she had come to West Fork in answer to an ad in our town newspaper, *The Fork Over Gazette*. City Hall was looking for someone to operate a hat and dress store here in West Fork. Jane loved to buy new outfits and she thought this would be just the right thing to have in town. I gave a groan because I wondered where we were going to put the tons of clothes she already had.

As the three of us walked over to the hotel, Jane gingerly leaned over and whispered in my ear that this lady had an angelic glow about her. I had not particularly noticed, but when Jane mentioned it I got the same feeling.

We went into the hotel and made sure that Jessica was checked in. Then I mentioned that I was getting hungry and told Miss Jessica that Jane and I wanted to treat her to supper. We knew it was too late to go to the ranch, so we checked into the hotel for the night, and would return to the ranch after church the next day.

We dined in the hotel restaurant and as we got to know Jessica, we learned she had been just about everywhere and done just about everything many times over.

"My last business venture was in Amarillo where I was the court stenographer," she explained. "I had the privilege of being present at all the well-known and famous outlaws' trials. Anyway, this one time when the jury announced their guilty verdict, the outlaw jumped up and screamed, 'I can't be guilty of murder because I'm Jesus Christ and He couldn't be guilty of murdering anyone because everyone knows that Jesus loves everybody!'

"The judge responded to the outlaw that everyone did know for a fact that Jesus loves everybody but that he wasn't Him.

"Well as the sheriff dragged the outlaw out of the court room, the convicted murderer was still hollering that they couldn't kill Jesus again and even if they did He would rise again and they would be sorry."

As we talked I got so caught up in the interesting conversation that I started remembering another very colorful individual whose name was Starr. So I asked Jessica if I could call her Belle Starr, and she said I could.

From this time on Jessica was always referred to as Belle Starr, the lady who would steal your heart. As a matter of fact, her new store was named Belle Starr's, and her motto was: "Come into my store and you'll leave as the belle of the ball with a star in your man's eye."

We asked Col. Dexter if some of the ranch hands and I could spend a few days the next week helping Belle stock her new store with the first shipment of dresses, hats, and accessories. We knew that Nancy would love to meet Belle and would be most helpful in adding her talents to decorating the store.

The next day, Sunday, Jane and I knew that the whole gang from the Delta D Ranch would be at church. This would be a perfect time to introduce Belle to the gang.

When we arrived, all the horseback riders and buckboard drivers started hollering as they welcomed Jane and me back. Col. Dexter was riding none other than Spirit the Wonder Horse, and next to him, the most beautiful palomino mare I had ever seen. While Jane and I were on our trip Col. Dexter had gone to a ranch about a hundred miles away and had bought the palomino mare. Her golden mane glistened like it had just been polished with some of Ol' Smokey's hair cream and you could almost see yourself in its shine. Jane took to her at first sight. We knew Spirit approved as he let out a whinny as if to say, "We did good."

Well we all piled into the church and Pastor Wells had already been briefed on all that had been going on around West Fork and he had a very timely message that everyone knew came directly from the Holy Spirit. Even Belle Starr was amazed to see all the love and reverence shown in the church.

Pastor Wells opened his sermon with a prayer of thanksgiving that God our everlasting Father had through the Holy Spirit sent His guardian angels to watch and protect and bring Jane and me back safe. He also thanked our heavenly Father for guiding Belle to West Fork and to bless her new business.

His sermon seemed to stand out more like a strong call for every Christian to seek with all his/her might a closer walk with the Lord. Pastor Wells closed by inviting all in attendance to come to the altar for a renewing and to, with His help, live more like Him starting today.

As everyone left there was not the usual noise and chatter but a sense of togetherness and love that had never been more evident than on this glorious morning.

As we all mounted for the trip back to the ranch not a single word was spoken the whole time, everyone was reflecting on the morning worship.

A hat or dress? If Belle don't have it,
you won't find it anywhere.

CHAPTER 13

The Uncloudy Days Trio Comes to West Fork

And Saul sent to Jesse, saying, "Let David now stand before me; for he has found favor in my sight." So it came about whenever the evil spirit from God came to Saul, David would take the harp and play it with his hand; and Saul would be refreshed and be well, and the evil spirit would depart from him. (NASV)
—1 Samuel 16:22-23

Howdy saddle pals, we've been keeping busy here at the Delta D Ranch these last few weeks, and the Lord's blessing of that additional fifteen hundred head of cattle has really added to the work on the ranch. The Bible says that with additional blessings comes additional responsibilities.

Well, we finally got the cattle on the train for shipment to the stockyards and everyone was back at the ranch wondering just what Col. Dexter had in store for us next.

As we approached the bunkhouse, we noticed a note tacked on the door from Col. Dexter. We all gave a disgruntled sigh because we knew that a big job was coming up and there was no time for rest. All the note said was that Col. Dexter wanted everyone in the barn now for a very special update.

"Uh, oh!" everyone exclaimed. This usually meant someone had made a mistake and punishment was eminent. One thing we knew about Col. Dexter was that he never chewed out anyone in front of the other ranch hands. This provided some comfort if you were the wrong-doer.

We wondered if Col. Dexter had heard some distressing news about Sparks McKinney who was up north visiting his father who was sick and not expected to live much longer.

Everyone was gathered around in the saddling area waiting for Col. Dexter and his news. As Col. Dexter and Ol' Smokey walked in we all studied their faces to determine the situation. There was absolutely no clue to Col. Dexter's expression, but there did seem to be a slight smile on Ol' Smokey's lips.

Col. Dexter walked to the front. We stood silently waiting for him to begin speaking. He cleared his throat but still seemed to be having trouble with his speech. By now we were all biting our fingernails as we anticipated Col. Dexter's next word. Finally he began.

"I don't know how to say this but something has showed up here on the ranch and it needs to be dealt with immediately," he said.

Everyone looked at each other and began to feel quite uncomfortable. All of a sudden Col. Dexter let out a hoop and a holler loud enough that he could be heard in the next county.

"You rowdies have done such a good and timely job and we are so far ahead of schedule that we are going to take a day off! I have tickets to attend the show featuring the Uncloudy Days Trio that you have been bugging me about ever since we heard that they were coming to West Fork and appearing at the opera house."

We were all so stunned, you could have heard a pin drop!

Then everyone asked in unison, "When, when?"

Col. Dexter replied that the trio was going to perform on the following Saturday night and we had front row seats.

By the time Saturday had rolled around you had never in your life seen a more greased up and smelled down bunch of rough riders than these cowboys were. Why you could smell them before you could see them.

Finally the time came to saddle up and start for town. Even Spirit the Wonder Horse was excited about going to town. He knew that he always got a special sugar cube every time we went to town on Saturday night.

When we rode into town Spirit headed for the livery stable that had his own stall and his special treat of sugar waiting for him.

Boy, was the opera house packed! Col. Dexter had added on the twelve former rustlers that had turned their lives over to Jesus and had asked Him to be their Savior. Well, with those twelve and us twelve, including Ol' Smokey and Col. Dexter, we filled up the whole front row. There was a line outside willing to buy our tickets at four times the price. We all just laughed and said, "You have all lost your ever-loving mind! There ain't enough money in this state to buy these tickets!"

We had just settled down in our great seats when the feller making the announcements stepped in front of the curtains and hollered that he had a few things to say before the performance. The place came alive and we thought we might have to rescue him if he tried to take away any of the time from the girls' show. All the announcer said was, "Here they are!"

As the curtains began to move apart we thought an earthquake had hit! The opera house began to shake and the hanging lamps started to swing because of the thundering applause. Everyone finally sat and quieted down.

Laura started out with an old fashioned, "Howdy, all!" And the roar once again shook the building.

The opening song was, "She'll Be Coming Around the Mountain When She Comes" and when the singers came to the verse "She'll be wearing pink pajamas when she comes," I thought the building was going to explode. The whistles, clapping, and hollering was deafening. What a show! The girls' music got better and better with each song.

Unfortunately the show had to come to a close. As the final selection, the wonderful Uncloudy Days Trio chose a favorite of mine, "Amazing Grace" and when they finished, that vast audience was standing as if they were beholding the presence of the Lord Jesus right there on stage with Laura, Emily, and Hannah. Without a doubt, this was the most beloved gathering I had ever experienced. I knew that the Holy Spirit had a hand in the planning of this great night of perfect and enjoyable entertainment to a bunch of rough men who spend many hours on lonely trails with none other than our Lord and Savior, Jesus Christ, leading our way.

Sunday morning we learned that Pastor Wells had extended the invitation for the girls to spend the night in the parsonage with his family. So with great surprise and joy we had the pleasure of seeing and hearing them sing again at our church the following morning. "Amazing Grace" rang through the rafters from the trio of angelic voices. In his sermon, Pastor

Wells said that to hear them sing reminded him how King Saul must have felt when David, inspired by the Holy Spirit, played his harp.

After the service, the majority of the congregation was at the train station to see Laura, Emily, and Hannah off. They waved goodbye as the train rattled off and disappeared around the bend. It was a sad moment because no one wanted the girls to leave.

With heavy hearts, we saddled up and started for the Delta D. We all knew that we had just seen a little bit of Heaven and we knew that there would be a next time either here or up there in the air where we would be with the great Uncloudy Days Trio once again.

The Uncloudy Days Trio blesses us
with their picking and singing.

W. Odell Mann

'Round the bend and out of sight!

CHAPTER 14

Sparks is Struck by Cupid's Arrow

And on the third day there was a wedding in Cana of Galilee, and the mother of Jesus was there; and Jesus also was invited, and His disciples, to the wedding. And when the wine gave out, the mother of Jesus said to Him, "They have no wine." And Jesus said to her, "Woman, what do I have to do with you? My hour has not yet come." His mother said to the servants, "Whatever He says to you, do it. Now there were six stone water pots set there for the Jewish custom of purification, containing twenty or thirty gallons each. Jesus said to them, "Fill the water pots with water." And they filled them up to the brim. And He said to them, "Draw some out now, and take it to the headwaiter." And they took it to him. And when the headwaiter tasted the water which had become wine, and did not know where it came from (but the servants who had drawn the water knew), the headwaiter called the bridegroom, and said to him, "Every man serves the good wine first, and when men have drunk freely, then that which is poorer; you have kept the good wine until now. This beginning of His signs Jesus did in Cana of Galilee, and manifested His glory, and His disciples believed in Him. (LB)

—John 2:1-11

Howdy saddle pals! Ya'll know I'm already hitched to my lovely bride, Jane, so this story's not about love finding me, but about love finding my good friend, Sparks McKinney.

You remember Sparks was up north visiting his sick father who, as it turns out, responded to his son's visit by getting well. Sparks was now returning to the Delta D Ranch a month later, and as you guessed it, he showed up right at supper time!

One day Sparks and I went to West Fork to get some supplies for Ol' Smokey and just as things would happen, we were coming out of the dry goods store just as our new school teacher Miss Helen Rambeau came out of Belle's hat and dress shop right across the street. When Sparks saw Miss Helen I think he lost his breath because he couldn't make a sound. Just about that time Miss Helen dropped one of the bags she was carrying and Sparks jumped off the porch and stumbled toward her. Would you believe that he fell the whole way across the street and finally came to rest on the ground right in front of Miss Helen?

It was a sight to behold seeing Sparks lying at Miss Helen's feet. Sparks, without missing a step, jumped up, brushed himself off, and picked up the bag. He just stood there like a love struck schoolboy as Miss Helen took the bag and walked on across the street.

Sparks is Struck by Cupid's Arrow

When I walked over to where Sparks was all he could say was, "She is the most beautiful girl that ever was born. Who is that gorgeous creature?"

I tried to tell him who she was but I don't think he heard a word I said because he had some kind of blank stare and a glassy look in his eyes. I could tell that cupid's arrow had found its target.

Well, Sparks, as you already guessed, wasn't worth very much the next week until he could get to town Saturday. Miss Helen was also quite stricken with her newfound hero and had been asking everyone who that young man was who fell at her feet. Needless to say, once the two met again, the romance was off to a flying start.

To Col. Dexter's delight, for the next few months everything at the ranch moved along smoothly.

One day Sparks borrowed the buggy from Doc Percy and brought Miss Helen by the Big House. The day happened to be Saturday so all the ranch hands were sorta sitting around doing nothing special. Sparks asked if it was okay for all the folks to gather around because he had something real important to say and he wanted his closest friends to hear it.

Col. Dexter was suspicious about what was going on, but finally said, "Certainly."

He then looked over at Nancy and told her to ring the dinner bell. The dinner bell wasn't used anymore to call for meals but for everyone to gather at a special announcement.

When all the ranch hands heard the bell they all came running to get the news. There was Sparks with a grin so broad it covered his whole face. Sparks took Miss Helen by the hand and begun to stumble over his words.

"Ya'll are the closest thing to being my family and I wanted to tell you first," he said. "I have asked Helen to marry me and also be my wife." He didn't even know what he was saying!

Sparks reached into his pocket and brought out a little blue box. He opened it and took out what we knew was a ring and started to place it on her finger. It was no one's surprise when he dropped it in the sand. Sparks looked like he was going to cry as he reached down and picked up the tiny and sparkling gold ring that looked like it had been made just for Helen's tiny hand.

As Sparks placed the ring on her finger he said, "With this ring I thee wed."

We all started to laugh! I told you that he didn't know what he was saying!

The next few weeks went by pretty smoothly as everyone was excited about the upcoming wedding. Jane wanted to do something special for the couple, so she insisted Helen borrow her wedding dress. Helen looked like a princess in the gown as she stood at the altar and Pastor Wells pronounced them husband and wife.

The whole congregation filed pass the newly wed couple, each one "ooing" and "awing."

Sparks is Struck by Cupid's Arrow

Col. Dexter hugged Helen and as he shook Sparks' hand he took something from his pocket and slipped it into Sparks' hand. Ol' Smokey later told us that it was two train tickets and money for a two-week honeymoon at the Fontana resort in the Great Smoky Mountains of North Carolina.

I watched the two as they boarded the train and the conductor called, "All aboard!" The train started to move and my memory traveled just a few months back when Jane and I were blessed with such an occasion. I was shaken back to reality by Jane tugging at

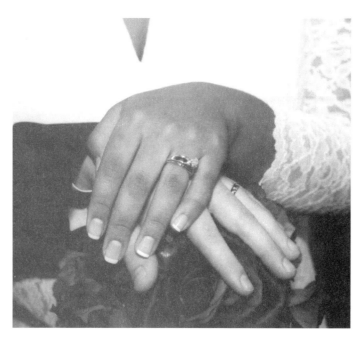

Now, Sparks, you can say ,"With this ring I thee wed."

my sleeve saying that it was time to get back to the Delta D.

On Sunday, Pastor Wells' sermon was taken from St. John's Gospel. He explained how Jesus had performed His first miracle at the wedding in Cana of Galilee. He said that nothing is more like the presence of Jesus than the marriage of two people as they let it be known that they have chosen each other forever.

Don't go far now, saddle pals, because there are many more good stories at the good ol' Delta D Ranch!

CHAPTER 15

'Round the Barnyard with the Ol' Cowpoke and Spirit's Son, Rags

*Let not your heart be troubled; ye believe in God
believe also in me. In my Father's house are many
mansions; if it were not so, I would have told you.
And if I go and prepare a place for you, I will come
again, and receive you unto myself; that where I am,
there ye may be also. (KJ)*
—John 14:1-3

Man, what a night that was when little Rags was born! We came close to losing the newborn son of Spirit the Wonder Horse. I don't believe I had ever seen rain pour as hard as it did on the night that Rags was born. The barn is only about a stone's throw from the bunkhouse but the rain was coming down so hard that I couldn't see it nor could I hear Spirit call out to me when he knew his little offspring was fixing to enter this world. I had Spirit in his stall and the mare that was carrying his son was in the stall right next to him. Spirit knew that something was wrong, and when I didn't come to his whinnying he knew that he had to get my attention somehow.

Meanwhile, I *had* heard the whinnying and sent Dusty to the Big House to have Col. Dexter call Doc Dowd, the veterinarian, and tell him to come out immediately.

By the time I reached Spirit, he was kicking the barn wall so hard that the boards started flying out from the wall. I guess if I had not gotten there when I did and calmed him down he would have kicked the whole barn down. As I got to the fallen mare I saw that she had severe chills and that if she didn't get warm soon she would die, but I didn't know what I could cover her with. There were plenty of quilts in the Big House but by the time I got them to the barn they would be soaked and would be no good to wrap a horse so cold as the mare was.

I began frantically trying to find something to use. I remembered that in the hayloft Ol' Smokey had stored some old rags that he had used winter before last to wrap a cow that was having a calf. I quickly climbed the ladder to the loft and began to throw the rags down.

When I got to the mare, lo and behold, there lay a newborn colt that was the spitting image of Spirit the Wonder Horse. He was just as white as new snow. I looked over at Spirit and he was prancing around like he knew that he was a father. My attention immediately went back to the mare and her needs. I started to wrap her with the rags and tried to get her warm, otherwise I knew she was a goner.

I looked around and suddenly I didn't see the new colt anywhere. I knew I had to find him soon or I would lose this beautiful colt.

As I was looking I happened to see the pile of rags slightly move over in the corner. I don't know how he did it, but somehow this newborn colt had wiggled his way inside this pile of rags and was completely invisible.

As I unraveled this bundle of white flesh from the rags I knew that this had to be his new name: Rags.

By this time old Doc Dowd had ridden up in his buggy and was completely soaked. Right away he began to work on the mare trying to get her warm. He even sent me to the ranch house to get some warm milk that was always kept in the kitchen. Doc Dowd thought that if he could get some of this into the mare that it might help get her temperature up. The poor mare was so weak at this point that she couldn't even drink the warm milk. I held her head up and we tried to get some of the milk down her throat but she was even too weak to swallow.

I looked over at Doc Dowd and he just shook his head. I knew that there was nothing more we could do. Spirit seemed to sense that the mare that had given him a son had died. Naturally it practically tore me up because this mare was one of Col. Dexter's favorites. He had raised her from a filly and had watched over and cared for her many nights as she lay near death with colic. Well, we knew that Doc Dowd had done all he could to save the mare's life, but he hated it as badly as we did.

When I went into the Big House to tell Col. Dexter the news, I could tell that he was in for a sleepless night. Nancy told me to have Doc Dowd come inside and change into some dry clothes. When he got in, she told him to warm himself by the fire and that she would pour him some hot tea. This, to him, was like a letter from home, so to speak. Nancy also insisted he stay the night.

Well, little Rags started growing as he responded to the personal care he got from all the people at the ranch, especially Ol' Smokey who used a nursing bucket he had made to feed the newborn calves and colts who had lost their mothers.

Even though Spirit was not a mother, you would have thought that he was by the way he took care and protected Rags around the ranch.

Sunday at service, Pastor Wells had prepared an encouraging word in his sermon and spoke about our loss and how he understood the pain we were all experiencing. He said that he couldn't back it up by Scripture but he personally believed that Rag's mother was watching down from horse heaven and enjoying the son she had brought into the world.

Well, saddle pals if you came by the Delta D Ranch any time now you would probably see Spirit the Wonder Horse and Rags, who is quite grown up now, kicking up their heels making an overall big show of themselves.

Young Rags, the spitting image of his father, Spirit the Wonder Horse.

CHAPTER 16

The Ol' Cowpoke Hammers Away with the Village Blacksmith

Pray ,too, that we will be saved out of the clutches of evil men, for not everyone loves the Lord. But the Lord is faithful; He will make you strong and guard you from satanic attacks of every kind. And we trust the Lord that you are putting into practice the things we taught you, and that you always will. May the Lord bring you into an ever deeper understanding of the love of God and of the patience that comes from Christ. (LB)
—II Thessalonians 3:2-5

Howdy saddle pals, come sit a spell with the Ol' Cowpoke and let me tell you another tall tale about a person that I think you will enjoy meeting.

It was last Saturday and I had saddled up Spirit to go into town to get some things that Jane had been bugging me about for days. I noticed that Spirit was limping a little bit and when I checked his hooves I found that one of his shoes was loose. I knew that I had to have it fixed today because a loose shoe can cause a bad sore and I surely didn't want that happening.

I went to the corral and threw a loop around the neck of one of the horses to hitch to the buckboard. You see, saddle pals; to throw a loop is the western way of saying to lasso an animal. I was not going to ride Spirit because my weight would cause his hoof to really get bad. After I had hitched up the buckboard and tethered Spirit to the tailgate, we started to town. I knew that we would have to take it pretty slow so as not to injure his foot any further.

It was afternoon when we finally got to West Fork and I went straight to the blacksmith shop where I knew Ol' J.C. Higgingbottom would be to take care of Spirit right away. Now one thing you can always count on is that Ol' Higgy, that's what everyone affectionately calls J.C., will be in his blacksmith shop on Saturday afternoon.

I got a little alarmed when he wasn't there and furthermore his forge was as cold as spring water. Now I really did get upset because this meant that Ol' Higgy had not been in his shop since yesterday. I went over to Belle's hat and dress shop and asked her if she had seen Ol' Higgy today.

"I haven't seen him since yesterday morning when I saw him going into Delmonty's about breakfast time," Belle told me.

Ol' Higgy was a regular boarder at Delmonty's which was owned and operated by Rosalie

Delmontico who is sorta sweet on Ol' Higgy, or at least he thinks so.

I left Spirit hitched to the rail and walked on over to Delmonty's. I was even more surprised at not finding Rosalie around. I saw Pastor Wells' horse, Brandy, hitched up in front of the church so I figured I would go in and ask if he had seen Ol' Higgy anywhere.

"As far as I know, Ol' Higgy should be in the blacksmith shop," Pastor Wells told me.

"Well he ain't nowhere around and nobody has seen hide nor hair of him since yesterday morning," I explained. "And furthermore, no one has seen Rosalie either." I really began to think that I had stirred up a hornet's nest.

I walked over to the general store where a game of checkers was always going on, to see if anyone had seen Ol' Higgy or Rosalie. Five or six fellows were just sitting around waiting to challenge the winner, but none of them had seen either of them anywhere.

As I was walking back to the shop where I had left Spirit tied up, I saw a small boy who I recognized as Jim Jr., the son of Jim Sexton, owner of the feed store down at the end of the street.

"Jim Jr., have you seen Ol' Higgy?" I asked him.

"The last time I saw him was about daybreak this morning," he said. "He was with Miss Delmontico and they were talking to a real rough looking fellow who carried a big shot gun. I couldn't get close enough to hear anything that was said but I saw Mr. J.C. take some money out of his pocket and give to the man. I don't know whether it's true or not, but it sorta looked like the man was holding the shotgun pointed at Mr. J.C."

"Well where'd they go?" I asked.

"The three of them walked off together and went into the boarding house and shut the door," Jim Jr. said. "You don't think the man was a robber or something and he wanted to hurt them, do you, Mr. Cowpoke?"

I wasn't sure. By now I was getting a little nervous and my mind began to play tricks on me. It's just like how Satan will always try to build fear in our minds and if he can get us to be fearful then he knows that our faith becomes smaller and smaller.

"I think we should begin to pray, Jim Jr." We bowed our heads and I continued. "We pray, dear Lord, that Ol' Higgy's and Miss Rosalie's guardian angels will protect them. And we ask the Holy Spirit to show us where they are and we ask this in the name of Jesus. Amen."

"Amen," Jim Jr. whispered.

"Now, Jim Jr., everything will be all right and don't you worry." You see, I was actually trying to convince myself.

I walked back over to the church and I met Pastor Wells just coming out.

"Any luck finding Ol' Higgy or Rosalie?" he asked.

I told him what Jim Jr. had told me and I would appreciate it if he would utter a prayer of agreement with me for their safety. Pastor Wells said that he would be glad to and that he wanted to give me a Scripture of encouragement. (Pastor Wells is never without his Bible.) He opened his Bible to Second Thessalonians 3:2-5 and read aloud.

You see, Pastor Wells already knew, by faith in the Holy Spirit, that Ol' Higgy and Rosalie were unharmed. Turned out I was the one who needed my faith strengthened and Pastor Wells knew that I needed to hear personally from the Lord through His Word that He was still in control and for me not to worry. You know, even I, the Ol' Cowpoke, felt that I had just been taken to the wood shed and that I had been given a gentle, but firm, spiritual spanking.

I went on into the boarding house to once again ask if anyone had seen Ol' Higgy or Rosalie today. There at the table was a rough looking fellow just finishing eating a plate full of Rosalie's delicious chicken stew.

I marched right over to the fellow and demanded, "Where did you take Ol' Higgy and Rosalie and what did you do to them?"

The fellow laughed and told me that they had given him twenty-five dollars if he would help them sneak away for a few minutes to go on a picnic. What a relief it was but you see, I had lost sight of the fact that worry is one of Satan's tools for getting us bound up. And if that happens, we start getting into doubt and losing faith. Saddle pals, don't ever let Satan get you to this point where he can cause your faith to get smaller through doubt and unbelief.

Well there you have it. Incidentally, the fellow's name was Chester Parsons and he was dressed like this because some friends had dared him to. You see, Chester was a millionaire wheat farmer from Kansas City and he just wanted to get away for a while without anyone recognizing him. Also, I led Chester to accept the Lord Jesus Christ as his Savior and he said that he would seek out a Bible-believing church when he returned to Kansas City. His parting remarks were, "I'll be seeing you again."

I put Spirit in a stall in the livery stable and jumped into the buckboard for the trip back to the Delta D. Uh, oh! I was so wrapped up in meeting Chester Parsons that I didn't get the things for Jane. Oh well! There's always Monday.

Hammering with Ol' Higgy.

CHAPTER 17

A Thousand Dollars for Sparks and Helen

*Jesus saith unto him, I am the way, the truth and
the life: no man cometh unto the Father, but by
me. If you had known me, ye should have known
my Father also: and from henceforth ye know
Him, and have seen Him. (KJ)*
— John 14:6-7

Howdy saddle pals! You'll never guess what, but
Sparks McKinney and his wife, Helen, are back from
their honeymoon already. Wow, how time flies here
at the Delta D Ranch! And much to their surprise,
Col. Dexter had redone the guest room for them un-
til a more ample place could be found for their resi-
dence.

Col. Dexter told Sparks that there was a line
shack a ways over about seven or eight miles from the
Big House. There was also two acres of prime
bottomland that would be a perfect spot for their
home. It wouldn't take but a little bit of work to
make the line shack a perfect little place for them to
live. Col. Dexter told Sparks that he could have the

shack and land for a thousand dollars. Col. Dexter also told him that there was a shooting contest that a new feed store was promoting and the prize was one thousand dollars for first place, but there was one problem, and that was Sparks had come down with pneumonia while on their trip. He had stopped by Doc Percy's and got some strong medicine that had really knocked him for a loop. The shooting contest was the following Saturday and Sparks said that he couldn't hit the side of a barn, that there was no way he could compete with other sharp shooters that soon. Sparks was really disappointed about this but there was no way that he could think of to be in the competition.

So I came up with a super idea and I bounced it off Col. Dexter. My idea was to let me do the shooting, after all, I did learn a thing or two from my wife, Jane Ryco, the world's greatest sharp shooter. And if I won the thousand dollars then Jane and I would make it a wedding present to Sparks and Helen.

Col. Dexter thought it was a super idea and he even offered to put up the entry fee of ten dollars.

Saturday came and all the hands showed up in support of the Ol' Cowpoke in this show of sharp shooting.

All the contestants lined up and prepared for the shoot out. The judge explained to us that the object of this event was to put five slugs into the vertical line leaving the space blank where the two lines crossed, three down from the top. Then four shots would make up the horizontal line with a space where the two lines crossed. The firearm for this shooting was to be a Colt 45 Peacemaker revolver. The first shot was to be forty feet from the target and each shot an additional foot. A total distance for the tenth, and final, shot would be fifty feet from the target. This shot had to complete the cross with the final shot to be in the space left at the spot where the two lines crossed. Ten shots made up the complete firing. The two lines that make up the cross must be perfectly straight without any waviness, and all the bullet holes most be equally spaced apart. We were reminded that it would be the judge's decision, as to who had the most accurate display of true marksmanship.

The first to shoot was Ol' Higgy, the blacksmith. He stepped up to the first line and took careful aim and fired. The hole cut dead center at the top of the up and down line. He stepped back a foot to the next line. All the shots following seemed to come into perfect place. For his final shot, the empty center space, looked like a cinch to be a perfect display but for some reason, it was off to the right.

The second shooter was Jason Jackson, the feed mill owner. Jason followed the same as Ol' Higgy for the first nine shots, but his tenth was also off to the right.

Coming up third was Race Hardmore who was another ranch owner just a few miles away. Race put his first nine shots in a perfect pattern, but his tenth or last shot missed the target completely.

The fourth man to shoot was Dennis Blackstone, the stagecoach driver. Dennis' first shot was a little to the left but all his other shots were in perfect position.

The next shooter was Max Caldwell, the local gunsmith whom everyone thought would be the winner. Max took careful aim and the bullet found its place just perfect. All the next eight shots were likewise in the right spot. You could tell by Max's expression he was thinking that they could start counting the thousand dollars even before his final shot. Max stepped to the line and cocked the hammer back, taking a careful and confident aim.

"Bang!" went the sound as the lead slug sped toward the target and the prize. When the judge examined the target there was no tenth bullet hole. Upon careful looking there was just enough lead stain to determine that his final shot had gone through the first hole. There was a groan as no one could believe his or her eyes. Max was just too confident.

It was finally my turn. I was so nervous I silently asked myself, what have I gotten myself into? Then it was almost like I could hear the Holy Spirit say to me, "Be still and know that I will never leave you nor forsake you. I won't do the shooting for you but remember you can do anything if you want to do it badly enough. You can do it for Sparks and Helen."

I looked over at Jane and she smiled and blew me a kiss. She mouthed the words "I love you" and "You can do it."

The first nine shots rang out and found their place perfectly forming two lines straight as an arrow. The final shot needed to be placed directly in the center, which would complete the cross and make me a winner.

As I took aim and was about to fire I glanced over to my right and there was Sparks and Helen. Sparks was supposed to be back at the ranch in bed but Helen had bundled him up real good, put him in the buckboard, and drove him to town because he said he had to go to the shooting match. I continued to take aim and squeezed the trigger. The air was pierced with the sound of gunfire. Everyone held his or her breath as the forty-five slug found its mark in the very place that it was supposed to go! The ground began to shake as the cheers and hand clapping and hats thrown into the air let it be known that the shot was perfect. Before I knew it everyone was shaking my hand and telling me how they knew it would be me all the time that done it.

The judge came over and brought the target with a perfectly formed cross. He had ten one-hundred-dollar bills in his hand and in shaking my hand said, "'Atta way to go champ! Here's your thousand dollars—one one-hundred-dollar bill for every shot."

Col. Dexter also came over and told me how proud he was of me and not to get too big-headed just because I could shoot at a piece of paper.

Sunday at church the first thing that came out of Pastor Wells' mouth was, "Well we have a new hero with us today. Maybe he will say a few words for us."

The only thing that I could think of to say was, "Praise God from whom all blessings flow!"

At the closing of his sermon, as always, Pastor Wells extended an invitation for anyone who wanted to accept Jesus as his or her Savior to come forward. The congregation stood and sang "If You Want Joy, Real Joy, Let Jesus Come into Your Heart."

Well you can imagine how much better Sparks felt when I handed the one thousand dollars over to him and told him to hurry up and get well because we needed his help on his new house.

Helen cooked a country dinner for all us cowboys working on the old line-shack, and we had ourselves a grand ol' time!

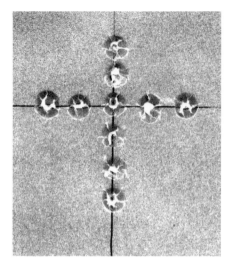

What a shot. A perfect 10!

Is that a big telegram Helen is sending to Sparks?

CHAPTER 18

'Round Town with the Ol' Cowpoke at Delmonty's Boarding House

*But when Paul had gathered a bundle of sticks
and laid them on the fire, a viper came out
because of the heat, and fastened on his hand.
And when the natives saw the creature hanging
from his hand, they began saying one to
another. "Undoubtedly this man is a murderer,
and though he has been saved from the sea,
justice has not allowed him to live." However,
he shook the creature off into the fire and
suffered no harm. (NAS)*
—Acts 28:3-5

Howdy saddle pals! As you know, I do most of my work around the Delta D Ranch here, but it wasn't long before I got the chance to take another trip into West Fork. Ol' Smokey had sent me to buy some supplies and as always, I was hungry. Ol' Smokey always is saying that we need to have a special fund set up just to pay for my vittles.

Well as I moseyed through town, I decided to stop in at Delmonty's, the boarding house. Rosalie always welcomes folks to come in for meal time, even if they aren't spending the night at the boarding house.

So I tied up Spirit outside and walked in the house to the smell of fresh biscuits and gravy. Rosalie had me sit at the head of the table and she started off by telling me and the other boarders about how earlier that day she went out back to the garden to get fresh vegetables for the supper meal.

"So as I bent down to start picking some tomatoes, I came to a complete halt because I thought I heard a noise that sounded like someone was shaking a baby rattle," she explained. "Now you know I'm not one who becomes unnerved easily but you have to admit that a baby rattle in a tomato patch is something strange!"

We all grinned, waiting in suspense for her to continue her story.

"Well, it turned out that it was something that rattled all right, but was not something that you would want to give to a baby. There in front of me was the biggest rattlesnake I had ever seen! I knew not to move, 'cause ya'll have told me that in your experiences with rattlesnakes, so I was hoping it would just go on off by itself and leave me alone. But that's not what the rattler wanted to do. As a matter of fact, the snake uncoiled and started toward me!

"I didn't have nothin' to defend myself, so I took a step backward and stepped on what I knew by the feel was a hoe. Then suddenly I remembered how much I'm always hollering 'bout people leaving tools out and not putting them where they belong. But this time I was grateful someone had not done what he was supposed to do!

"Being careful not to make any sudden move, I bent down and picked up the hoe and made a short work of this giant varmint. Then I just went on picking my vegetables and prepared the meal for all you diners." Rosalie smiled about her heroic story and we all laughed.

After the meal was over, all the folks went on about how good everything was and especially the delicious meat that she had cooked. We all wanted to know just what it was. Rosalie, in her special charm, said that it was a special dish that Ol' Smokey had sent her and told her to try out. Of course I knew what the truth was because one of Ol' Smokey's favorite dishes was roasted rattlesnake. Now I don't know and I can't say for sure whether the Holy Spirit had brought that hoe and put it where Rosalie could step on it or what but I believe that He did.

As usual the Holy Spirit had already spoken to Pastor Wells and had given him his sermon topic and Scriptural reference. His opening remarks on Sunday were that the Holy Spirit was in the people protecting business and that he understood that there was a certain lady in the congregation that knew first hand what this was all about.

Pastor Wells related to us how every believer is under the watch care of his own guardian angel who is under the special assignment from the Holy Spirit to protect him in his time of danger.

Well saddle pals, I hope you remember how much Jesus loves you and that your guardian angel is always with you!

Is Rosalie thinking about Higgy or preparing her next meal?

You better run varmint! The stew pot's coming!

CHAPTER 19

The Ol' Cowpoke Becomes Sheriff for a Day

Yea, though I walk through the valley of the shadow of death, I will fear no evil: for thou art with me; thy rod and thy staff they comfort me. (KJV)
—Psalms 23: 1-4

Howdy saddle pals! This tale, as you will soon see, is quite different from the usual ones. The Ol' Cowpoke got himself into a little bit of a jam that for a while even he didn't know where he was in. It all happened just last Friday when Sheriff Ben Cassidy was out at the Delta D and all of us cowhands were swapping yarns and doing a little bit of bragging about how we each have spent much time breaking wild horses. We began showing off the battle scars from the times that we got throwed off. I even had quite a number as I rolled up my sleeves and invited everyone to take a look.

Sheriff Ben was standing over to one side and all the bragging kinda got the best of him and he hollered out with somewhat of a snicker, "You sissies that call yourselves rugged cowboys I bet don't have any horse on this ranch either broken or not that I can't ride bare back, do ya?"

Sheriff Ben invited me, the Ol' Cowpoke, to go to the corral and pick out one.

"I'll show you tenderfeet what riding is all about," he told me.

I was a little nervous about Sheriff Ben's request, but at his insistence, I threw my lariat on a young mare that Sparks had about half broken and brought her to the breaking corral. I asked Ben if he was sure he wanted to ride without a saddle. Ben chuckled and grabbed the rein and a handful of mane and with one giant leap was aboard. For a second the mare, which we had given the name Mighty Molly, just stood there and we wondered if she was going to move at all. All of a sudden Molly started to shake and every inch of her body began to quiver. She took a leap straight up with all four hoofs clearing the ground. When she touched the ground she started to spin like a cyclone and before we knew what was going on Sheriff Ben went airborne and landed flat on his back on the other side of the rail fence. Sheriff Ben lay there motionless and everyone ran to his assistance.

We could tell that Sheriff Ben had hit the ground mighty hard and we were concerned that he might have injured his back. Since all of us ranch hands were born-again believers and baptized in the

Holy Spirit, we gathered around the sheriff and laid hands on him and began claiming in agreement that Sheriff Ben's back was not injured and that he was healed in the name of Jesus. Sheriff Ben still had not moved because he was knocked out colder than last week's mackerel. I raced to the Big House and told Col. Dexter what had happened and asked if it was okay if I called Doc Percy to get him over here pronto.

"Just do it," Col. Dexter said. "You don't have to get my permission to get attention for a hurt man."

I went to the phone, called Doc Percy, and asked him to come quick.

It seemed like forever but it really was in no time at all before Doc Percy was pulling up in his doctoring buggy. He grabbed his bag and made his way to where everyone was gathered around Sheriff Ben and still praying over his motionless body. Doc Percy started examining Sheriff Ben between all the hands that were still laid on him. Doc Percy reached into his bag and brought out an ammonia capsule, crushed it, and began to wave it under Sheriff Ben's nose. With a cough, Sheriff Ben started to revive and tried to get up.

"No! No! I want to check for possible back injury before you move around," Doc Percy said.

Ol' Smokey came in with a blanket and laid it down.

"Now, I need a couple people's help to gently roll Sheriff Ben over onto this blanket," Doc Percy said.

We did as he said and rolled Sheriff Ben over onto his stomach so his back and spine could be checked. By this time Sheriff Ben was fully awake and was able to respond to Doc Percy and explain where he hurt. After much probing around and pressing on Sheriff Ben's back, Doc looked up and excitedly exclaimed that his back was not broken, just badly bruised.

"Praise God that He answered our prayers!" we all said in unison.

"Looks like Sheriff Ben's gonna be okay," Doc Percy said.

"Yea!" we all shouted.

"Now even though Sheriff Ben's not seriously injured, I still want him to take it easy for at least a week," Doc Percy instructed.

Sheriff Ben then asked me if I would drive him home to West Fork in the buckboard and tie his horse, Silver Lady, to the back because he was too sore to ride horseback. Of course he knew I would be glad to do so. As soon as we pulled up to Sheriff Ben's house he remarked how strange it was that his thirteen-year-old daughter, Beverly, didn't run out to meet him. Usually whenever she heard hoof beats she would run and throw her arms around Sheriff Ben's neck and excitedly tell him, "I love you,

Daddy." Then she would jump up on Silver Lady and ride the rest of the way with Sheriff Ben.

This time however, she was nowhere in sight. I pulled the buckboard up to the hitching rail and started to help Sheriff Ben down. Sheriff Ben's wife, Debbie, busted out of the door screaming that she had just received a call from a man telling her that if she ever wanted to see Beverly alive again that her husband would have to let the prisoner he was holding out of jail. Sheriff Ben was holding Jake Puckett for the marshal to come take him to Dodge City to stand trial for rustling. It had been Jake's brother, Slim, who called and she was scared almost out of her mind.

Debbie then noticed that her husband was not riding his horse and that he looked like he was hurting. Sheriff Ben explained what happened but that he was not seriously hurt. Sheriff Ben told her that the important thing now was not him but finding Beverly.

"CP, I don't know if I can ride with all the pain I have," Sheriff Ben told me. "I'll have to make you temporary sheriff so you can ride out and find my daughter."

"Me?" I asked in surprise.

Just then, Johnny Sampson, a neighbor, rode up.

"Sheriff Ben!" he called out. "I was on my way home from school when I saw Beverly taken captive by some man."

"Did you see where they went?" I asked.

"They were entering Rimrock Canyon last I saw," Johnny said.

"Start there," Sheriff Ben told me.

Johnny was shaken up pretty badly so Debbie took him into the house to try to calm him.

"I'll start at Rimrock Canyon and see if there is anything I can find to point to Beverly's whereabouts," I told Sheriff Ben. "But first I need to call the ranch and speak to Col. Dexter to let him know about Beverly."

Col. Dexter said to do what I could to find Beverly, but insisted I keep him informed.

The ranch was on one of the trails to Rimrock Canyon so I took the buckboard back and picked up Spirit the Wonder Horse. By this time it was getting late so I coaxed Spirit into a full gallop so I could reach Rimrock Canyon before dark. The sky looked like rain and I didn't want any tracks that might be there to be washed away. Spirit and I arrived at Rimrock Canyon just as the sun was disappearing behind the hilly range. I started to search the area for any signs that might be helpful. Since town, I had been praying and asking the Holy Spirit to guide me and show me anything that might be helpful in locating Beverly. I must have covered a square mile and the sun was quickly setting. I was getting anxious about Beverly's safety and frantically began to call upon the Holy Spirit to reveal anything that I might have missed in my search. All of a sudden I spotted something that made my heart skip a beat and I knew right then where Beverly was being held captive.

I raced back to town and to Sheriff Ben and Debbie's house and burst in without even knocking.

"I know where she is!" I bellowed out. "Praise God, I know where she is being held!"

"Hallelujah!" Debbie shouted.

"Give me about three hours and I'll have Beverly back home," I said.

"Oh, no, you don't," Sheriff Ben said. "I'm coming with you if it kills me to get in the saddle!"

As soon as Sheriff Ben got his horse, Silver Lady, he bounced onto her back and exclaimed, "Let's go!"

In full gallop we started north and about nine o'clock we arrived at the place I was looking for. Just inside the county line there was an old abandoned shack that had not been used for such a long time that vines had covered it over.

Sheriff Ben and I dismounted and left Spirit and Silver Lady about three hundred yards from the shack. As we approached we could detect a faint glimmer of light coming through the vines. Sheriff Ben's pains had become so intense that he told me I would have to go the rest of the way alone because he might make a sound that would endanger Beverly's life. I told Sheriff Ben to go back to the horses and keep them quiet. I got right up close to the shack wall and gently pulled the vines apart so I could see the light of a small lamp that was inside. I quickly scanned the interior. Lying in a corner all huddled up was Beverly. She was bound hand and feet with a gag around her head.

As I continued to scan the room I saw the figure of a man leaning back in a chair against a wall. He looked to be asleep. I eased over to where the door was. The fellow had cleared away the vines and I was able to get inside.

As I bolted through the door with my pistol drawn the guy inside got up out of his chair drawing his gun at the same time. I fired my Colt Peacemaker and his weapon flew into many pieces as my slug found its mark slamming his shattered gun against the wall. We, on the Delta D, were trained to disarm, not to kill.

The outlaw bolted for the door and I grabbed the chair and threw it in front of him, causing him to stumble and hit his head on the wall, knocking him out cold.

While he was out I took the rope off Beverly and tied the outlaw's hands and feet like a bulldogged steer. I went to Beverly's side and tried to reassure her she would be okay, I removed the gag. Then I helped Beverly to her feet and she started sobbing.

"Thank you, Jesus! Thank you, Jesus!" was all she could say.

"There's someone outside waiting to see you, Beverly," I told her.

When Sheriff Ben heard the shot he couldn't wait any longer and made his way down to the cabin.

Then when Beverly saw her father she ran to him and hugged him so hard that he almost fainted in pain.

As acting sheriff, I arrested the outlaw and draped him over his saddle and placed him behind bars in the cell beside his brother.

Finally we returned to Sheriff Ben's house about midnight and found Debbie still pacing, as she had been when we left.

When she saw Beverly, she shouted out, "Thank you heavenly Father! Thank you heavenly Father!"

We all went into the house and Debbie poured us a cup of coffee. Beverly excused herself though and said that all she wanted was a bath.

Sheriff Ben turned to me and asked, "CP, there is one thing I want to know. What did you find out at Rimrock Canyon that let you know where Beverly was being held?"

I laughed. "Do you remember last July when we went out hunting and were held up in that little abandoned shack due to the pouring rain? There was that creek bank at the back of the shack where we saw a holly tree with red leaves and the leaves were as red as the berries."

"That's right, the red tree that looked like it was on fire!"

"Well, when I was searching for clues at Rimrock Canyon, I came across a bunch of horse tracks and lying amidst the tracks was a red holly leaf.

Now I don't know whether the outlaw had brought it there in his clothes or whether the Holy Spirit had dropped it there for me to find, but in either case it was His doing and as always He is on the spot."

That Sunday, as usual, Pastor Wells had something to say about our adventures.

"The Holy Spirit has done it again!" he exclaimed.

There you have it saddle pals, the time I was sheriff for a day. Sheriff Ben is back now fully recovered and all is well at the Cassidy household. I had to turn in my sheriff's badge but that's okay.

There is the vine-covered shack, but Beverly is safe at home.

Sheriff Cowpoke sez that crime does not pay.

CHAPTER 20

Just Foolin' Around with the Ol' Cowpoke and Ol' Betsy the Guitar

*Therefore said he unto them, The harvest truly is
great, but the labourers are few: pray ye therefore
the Lord of the harvest, that he would send forth
labourers into his harvest. Go your ways: behold, I
send you forth as lambs among wolves.
Carry neither purse, nor scrip, nor shoes:
and salute no man by the way.
And into whatsoever house ye enter, first say, Peace
be to this house. And if the son of peace be there,
your peace shall rest upon it: if not,
it shall turn to you again.
And in the same house remain, eating and drinking
such things as they give: for the labourer is worthy
of his hire. Go not from house to house. (KJV)*
—Luke 10:2-7

Well howdy saddle pals! Last Saturday was a blister
so after breakfast I was just sitting out in front of the
bunkhouse plunking a way on my guitar, Ol' Betsy,

when Ol' Smokey came running over to me and told me that the Col. wanted to see me right away. Ol' Smokey gets a kick out trying to make me think that the Col. is mad at me about something. Well I humored him a little by pretending that I was nervous and I hurried to the Big House to see if the Col. really wanted to see me. Well, it turned out that he really did want me, not to chew me out but to ask me to play my guitar at a get-together he was planning the next Saturday. Col. Dexter said that he had meant to speak to me about this ever since he heard me play. Of course, being the shy, bashful type that I am, I tried to convince him to ask Ol' Smokey to play his harmonica instead. I told Col. Dexter that Ol' Smokey would be pleased to furnish the entertainment for the party.

"Thanks, but no thanks," Col. Dexter said. When Col. Dexter asks there is no way around but to give in to his wishes.

When the day arrived the people started coming from miles around and the place that was prepared for the occasion wouldn't hold them all. Col. Dexter told us to start cleaning out the saddling area between the stables in the barn. Our barn is not a typical barn. When you start walking from one end to the other you wish you had packed a lunch. Well all of us ranch hands grabbed brooms and started to get the place cleaned up. Col. Dexter said he wanted the place ready by the time the guests walked over from the Big House.

Just Foolin' Around with the Ol' Cowpoke and Ol' Betsy the Guitar

As soon as the place was shining, some of the cowboys climbed up into the hayloft and started throwing down bales of hay to use as seats. The guests began to fill up the new meeting hall and before you could say "horse feathers" the barn was standing room only.

Col. Dexter came to the platform that we had fashioned from some lumber we had lying around. Everyone applauded Col. Dexter and he pretended that this wasn't necessary, but we all knew that he was eating it up. Col. Dexter said that he wanted all the people there to meet the new faces that had joined the ranch and West Fork since the last time he had a shindig like this, which was about three years prior.

The first one he called up for introduction was Nancy. Col. Dexter told us that Nancy had come all the way from Denver just to help him set his house in order. It was about three years prior that Col. Dexter's wife, Nell, had caught some kind of fever and all our care and prayers could not save her. It turned out that Nancy was the daughter of a long-time friend of Col. Dexter who had written him that Nancy was the victim of a jealous husband who kept her black and blue from his constant beatings. Nancy had tried everything she knew to hang on because she believed that marriage was forever but things had gotten so bad that she couldn't stand it any longer. Col. Dexter said that Nancy has a home here on the Delta D Ranch for as long as she wants.

The next introduction was the hat and dress store owner, Belle Starr. Belle had stepped off the train just to stretch her legs and talk to the mayor. She was on her way to some city up north and was so impressed with West Fork that she bought a quaint little building and opened her own hat and dress store. Incidentally, Col. Dexter said that her business was doing quite well and she was enjoying our unusual little town more and more.

Col. Dexter then called Sparks McKinney to the front and made a formal welcome to him as a permanent part of the ranch and it's operation. Sparks McKinney had come to the bunkhouse unexpectedly one night and was asked to make a decision whether he would come back to the Delta D and be our bronc buster. Sparks had gotten word from his family up north that his father was seriously ill and he needed to come home immediately if he wanted to see his father alive. Well, saddle pals before Sparks left for his family's home all the cowboys gathered around him, laid hands on him and I, the Ol' Cowpoke, was asked to pray for Spark's father and for a good report when he got home. I, along with the rest of the fellows, prayed in agreement that Spark's father would be healed and restored to his original health. Well when Sparks arrived home, whom do you suppose met him at the door? It was none other than Spark's father himself, fit as a fiddle, praising the precious name of Jesus. Sparks believes to this day that everything that happened was a divine plan of our heavenly Father to get him to the ranch to become one of us. We sincerely believed this. Sparks returned and is now our official horse breaker and absolutely loves his job. Sparks had a whirlwind romance with our schoolteacher, Miss Helen Rambeau, who incidentally became his wife.

Col. Dexter then called to the front our new physician, Doctor Percy Wiltingham, affectionately called Doc Percy. I believe that Doc Percy was brought to West Fork by the Holy Spirit just to aid in the life-threatening bout with the black widow spider, which almost took my life.

Although he needed no introduction, our own Pastor Wells and his wife Rachel and son Jamie were welcomed next. It is almost impossible to imagine not having Pastor Wells with us. Since Pastor Wells' arrival we have been led into a much deeper understanding and working of the Holy Spirit. It was Pastor Wells who performed the wedding ceremony of the beautiful bride Jane Ryco and me the Ol' Cowpoke.

"Since we're on the subject of newly married couples, there's an announcement that needs to be made," Col. Dexter said. "Jane and CP come up here."

We did as we were told.

"I think that you've stayed in the penthouse apartment long enough so you're being evicted," he said.

The penthouse was what everyone called the attic where all the unused articles were stored. You see, Col. Dexter was a pack rat and nothing was ever thrown away. Needless to say, I was confused and I glanced at Jane.

"So since you don't have a place to live, something has to be done about it," the Col. continued. "Mr. and Mrs. Cowpoke, you know the grassy knoll just over the rise on the far side of the fishing pond that you have always admired? The place where you officially proposed to Jane? Well, I have purposely kept you from that area until today. The boys have completed, furnished, and Nancy has hung drapes in your new house. You, Jane, remember last week when Nancy asked you to go with her to town and with the help of Belle had picked out the colors and patterns for the drapes which you had been led to believe were for the Big House? Well, Jane and CP here are the keys to your new house, with the deed to five acres of the best bottom land around, along with our best wishes to you both.

"I am now promoting you to foreman of the Delta D Ranch. I have been very proud of your work these years and you deserve this promotion. Incidentally CP, you don't have to perform for us today on the guitar because, you see, I have heard you play."

What a blessing this was for Jane and me! The Lord just keeps right on blessing and blessing His children!

Pastor Wells couldn't wait for Sunday to tell us his always timely encouraging remarks. He related to us that God's Word tells us that His eyes are always going to and fro looking for ways to bless His children and that He loves you and me so much. Pastor Wells, with what looked like a shiny spot under each eye began to tell us how much his coming to West Fork had meant to him and his family but his words were drowned out by the cheers and applause that he finally just shut up and gave a look of humility.

Col. Dexter shouted from the pew, "God really outdid himself when He brought you, Pastor Wells, to West Fork."

Now we don't argue with the Word.

CP is all ready to play for Col. Dexter's shindig.

CHAPTER 21

'Round the House Looking for Nancy

*Pray all the time. Ask God for anything in line
with the Holy Spirit's wishes. (LB)*
—Ephesians 6:18

Well howdy saddle pals! It was just the other day I
was telling you about Nancy Peterson who came to
us under some very heartbreaking times. She had
quite a violent husband. Even though Col. Dexter
owns the whole spread, most of the daily decisions
are left in the hands of Nancy. She was the daughter
of a good friend of Col. Dexter and she came from a
pretty far away place. Nancy takes charge of the gen-
eral operation of the ranch dealing with everything
except those concerning the cowboys and their du-
ties. She does such a fantastic job keeping everything
in order that things seem to get done on their own. It
is almost as if she is invisible. Matter of fact, that's ex-
actly what happened just a short time ago when the
telephone rang and Nancy, who usually answers,
didn't do so.

Col. Dexter, who happened to be passing through, answered and it was the general store in West Fork calling for Nancy about an order she had made. Thinking that she must have stepped over to the mess hall to ask Ol' Smokey a question, Col. Dexter told the clerk he would have Nancy call back.

Col. Dexter walked over to the mess hall to give Nancy the message but much to his surprise no one had seen Nancy since yesterday. Col. Dexter found this quite strange and not a bit like Nancy. He called in all the ranch hands that were not on the range to start looking for Nancy. Everyone knew that she must be somewhere close by because her horse, Wonder Woman, was still in her stall.

Out back was an old dinner bell that was now used for calling Nancy if she was not nearby. The ringing came with no success.

By now there was fright in everyone's eyes and all kinds of thoughts started piling into their minds. Col. Dexter knew that they must not give the devil any foothold by allowing fear to invade their minds. Col. Dexter made a call to Pastor Wells and told him to get in touch with the prayer partners and start intercessions for Nancy and her safety.

Pastor Wells wasted no time starting prayers from all directions and the word spread very rapidly. Many of the town's folk from West Fork started pouring in at the ranch to help in the search for Nancy. The search continued throughout the night but with no encouragement.

'Round the House Looking for Nancy

About ten o'clock the next morning Pastor Wells' wife, Rachel, suggested that everyone gather in the room where Nancy was last seen and join hands and pray silently asking the Holy Spirit to reveal the whereabouts of Nancy and that she be all right.

Everyone responded and soon the room was completely silent. In the quietness of the room one of the ladies spoke up and said that she thought she heard a voice coming from the floor. Everyone dropped down on their knees and put their ears to the floor.

In the middle of the floor was a trap door leading to a cellar that had been used for storing canned foods back when Mrs. Dexter was still living. She used to raise a giant garden and canned most of the vegetables. The only way to get down to the cellar was through the trapdoor. Once the door was opened a ladder that was tied to a rope had to be brought up and leaned against the door to keep it from closing. If this ladder was not securely leaning against the door it would close thereby trapping anyone who might be in the cellar.

The old trapdoor, as heavy as it was, finally was raised enough to peer inside. Mrs. Wells called out Nancy's name. A faint voice replied, "yes." No other sound came up and the men grabbed the door and raised it fully open so that a light could shine down. There on the damp floor was Nancy's listless body. She had screamed so long trying to get someone's attention that she was completely exhausted and half frozen.

By this time the ranch hands were returning from the range. They saw the crowd standing outside of the Big House door and came over to see what was going on.

"What is it, Rachel?" I asked.

"Nancy's trapped in the cellar and we don't know if she's even alive!" she cried.

By this time Col. Dexter was almost out of his mind with worry so Pastor Wells walked with him into the next room to settle him down.

I pushed everyone aside and almost jumped down into the cellar without the help of the ladder. I picked Nancy up and toted her to where she could be raised through the trapdoor. The ranch hands lifted her out and carried her into the sitting room and laid her on the couch.

The entire crowd started to pray and lay hands on Nancy asking our heavenly Father to grant our petition for her full recovery. She was as pale as a sheet and so cold. One of the ladies had gone into the bedroom and had brought a quilt and covered Nancy so she could get warm.

The prayer vigil was kept up for the rest of the day and into the night. About twelve-thirty in the morning Rachel shouted, "Look! Nancy's color is returning!"

Pastor Wells went over to Nancy's side and put his hand on her forehead and exclaimed excitedly,

"Praise the precious name of Jesus, she's going to be all right!"

The next few days everything went pretty much back to normal around the ranch and Nancy got back her strength and once again took her rightful place on the Delta D. When Nancy's strength had returned I asked her how she got trapped in the cellar.

"I had never been down in the cellar before and I thought that it might be a good place to store supplies since it was so cold down there and would keep fresh things from spoiling," she said. "I blocked the trapdoor with the ladder like it was supposed to be and went down. In the dark, somehow I tripped over the ladder and it fell and the door slammed shut. I started to scream but no one could hear me, I guess. After a while I was so weak that I must have passed out and when I came to, I heard talking upstairs and I called out as loud as I could and I guess that's when the prayer group, in its quiet time, was able to hear me. Praise God!"

Sunday in Pastor Wells' sermon he was all primed to tell us how close we came to losing Nancy, and we were reminded again how much we have to lean on the Holy Spirit and never be out of touch with Him, especially since there is a real devil out there trying to destroy God's children. He said that he believes that the Holy Spirit had inspired Rachel to have a quiet time and that's how Nancy was able to be heard. We must always be in an attitude where our spirit is listening to hear what the Holy Spirit is saying.

Pastor Wells encouraged the congregation to always be sure that they pray within the will of God and a good way to be sure is to pray in the Holy Spirit.

That winning smile lets you know how important Nancy is around the Delta D.

CHAPTER 22

Sister Susan and her Old Fashioned Revival

*To Him alone doeth great wonders for His
mercy endureth forever. (KJV)*
—Psalms 136:4

Well howdy all you young saddle pals! Are you ready
to jaw a spell? Every once in a while I meet someone
while on the trail that seems to defy all reasoning.
Just such an occasion happened about a week ago
right about dusk. We had just gathered around the
campfire for a soothing cup of coffee, having made
sure the cattle and horses were settled for the night.
Yes, saddle pals, they have to be tucked in also.

We were jawing back and forth wondering how
to spend the time until everyone fell asleep. We
couldn't hear a thing but the gentle lowing of the cat-
tle. All of a sudden in the light of our campfire was
the most unusual sight one could imagine. We all
rubbed our eyes to see if we had dropped off to sleep
and were dreaming. But we were not. There in the
night, visible only by the flickering of the campfire,

was a covered wagon being driven by a tiny beautiful lady dressed all in white. Amazingly she had approached without disturbing the cattle. Her white dress had a glow that looked almost ghostly. It was a sight to behold. None of us were frightened; we just kept staring. On the side of the wagon was what looked like a banner and written on it were the words, "Jesus is the only way." The little lady finally spoke as she looked down on us and her smile was so beautiful that I could have sworn that we were looking at an angel.

"Howdy all!" she exclaimed. "Well by those puzzled faces I'd imagine ya'll want to hear more about me, huh?"

"Yes, ma'am," some of us answered.

A couple of cowboys walked over to the wagon and helped our newfound friend down and spread out a saddle blanket for her to sit on. Our angel could tell by our puzzled looks that we wanted to know more about her.

"I'm Susan Jacobs, a travelin' evangelist. I just spent the last seven years under the mentorship of Great Katherine!" None of us had heard of such a lady.

"What are you doing out this way?" a ranch hand asked.

"Well I'm headed to the little town of West Fork, Kansas."

Sister Susan and her Old Fashioned Revival

One of the ramrods hollered out, "The Holy Spirit has struck again!" (Cowboys don't know how to say things gently, they just blurt it out.)

Susan kind of looked startled to hear a dusty cowboy from this rugged place refer to the Holy Spirit.

"Sorry, ma'am," I began, "but we all are Jesus people and we wouldn't leave home without Him."

"Praise Jesus! I just got me a telegram from the West Fork minister who wants me to come in and hold an old fashioned revival!"

This was the most unbelievable tale we had ever heard!

We all said in unison, "She's talking about Pastor Wells."

"That is exactly who sent the telegram!" Susan said.

I asked Susan to stay with the trail herd because we would be heading toward West Fork in about two days and she shouldn't be going alone out on the trail. Besides, we would welcome a pleasant bit of company for the remainder of the drive. I had already thought that Col. Dexter and Nancy would really enjoy meeting Susan and hearing all about her ministry. I was also looking forward to introducing Susan to Jane.

The next two days were a joy as we had a chance to eat real cooking and not Ol' Smokey's burnt vittles. I'm kidding, Ol' Smokey is a good cook and we enjoy his corny humor.

W. Odell Mann

The time passed quickly and before we knew it we could see the ranch over yonder. I rode on ahead to prepare Col Dexter for the forthcoming treat. As the cowhands herded the cattle into the fenced area for new stock, I jumped onto the wagon and drove it over to the barn where the horses could be watered, fed, and put into a stall.

By this time Nancy had come running and had already helped Susan down off the wagon before I had a chance to do so.

"You must be Susan, whom CP tried to tell me about," Nancy said. "He was so excited I barely could understand what he was trying to say!"

They hugged like two friends who had not seen each other for a long time.

Susan fit in perfectly and she was put up in the guest room so she could rest. We promised to take her to town the next day.

Nancy went to the telephone and called Pastor Wells to tell him that we had a visitor that had come from a long way to meet him and would love to see him tomorrow. Exactly one hour and thirteen minutes later Pastor Wells and Sister Rachel were pulling into the yard.

By this time Susan had freshened up a bit and once again looked like an angel. For the rest of the day and into the night it was like a great reunion for the five of them. Col. Dexter, Miss Susan, Nancy, and the Wells' had bonded together to form a lasting friendship.

126

Sister Susan and her Old Fashioned Revival

Sunday morning Pastor Wells was like a little boy at Christmas time. He was all aglow when he introduced Evangelist Susan Jacobs to the congregation and let them know that she, along with the Holy Spirit, had brought an old fashioned revival to West Fork and would be staying as long as He decided.

The revival was a great success bringing many of God's children into His fold and encouraging each of us to walk in the way of the Lord.

Sister Susan takes her sword in hand.

You can almost hear people singing from the West Fork chapel!

CHAPTER 23

A Little Taste of Heavenly Delight!

*Bring all the tithes into the storehouse so that
there will be food enough in my temple; if you
do, I will open up the windows of heaven for
you and pour out a blessing so great you won't
have room enough to take it in! "Try it! Let me
prove it to you! Your crops will be large, for I
will guard them from insects and plagues.
Your grapes won't shrivel away before they
ripen," says the Lord of hosts. And all nations
will call you blessed, for you will be a land
sparkling with happiness. These are the
promises of the Lord of hosts. (LB)*
—Malachi 13:10-12

Howdy saddle pals! You caught me drinking a large
glass of cold milk! Yum, yum! You could probably say
that a glass of cold milk is the favorite drink of us
cowboys, and the ladies too. Back when Ol' Smokey
was cook he always kept a jar, or jug as he called it, of
milk handy for the cowboys to have a glass when we
are on the trail. Now that Col. Dexter made Ol'
Smokey manager of the ranch and hired Blake to re-

place him as trail cook, Blake is doing the same thing with keeping milk on the trail. I never learned the secret of how Ol' Smokey kept the milk cold while out on the trail, but he did. Ol' Smokey must have shared his secret with Blake because it's always cold.

One day when Ol' Smokey was going after a supply of milk from the dairy farm he asked Blake to go along to learn the way and he invited me, the Ol' Cowpoke, to go along too. You will probably find it somewhat strange that I didn't know where the dairy was nor had I ever been there.

We hitched up the covered wagon because shade was needed to keep the sun off the milk cans. I saddled up Spirit the Wonder Horse, and Blake took his big red sorrel and we were ready to go. It was early, about five thirty in the morning when we started out. We needed to start then because the dairy farm was about sixty miles away. We could only go about ten miles per hour, which made it around twelve o'clock when we got there.

When we pulled up to the cooling shed, which was called a shed even though the place had been dug into the ground about twenty feet deep and made into a room about thirty feet square, a bouncy, bibbed-overall dressed lady called Annette, met up with us.

Annette always met Ol' Smokey at the shed when he came by. As always, she had a big glass of extremely cold milk waiting for him when he pulled up. Ol' Smokey jumped down from the wagon and stretched because he had been riding for about six hours. Blake and I dismounted and did a couple of jumps to limber up a bit.

"Come on, ya'll, I have something I want you to see that wasn't here the last time Ol' Smokey came to my farm," Annette said.

She took us to a big, well-built building that looked more like a horse barn than something you would find on a dairy farm. Annette handed us each a coat, telling us that it was pretty cold inside. We didn't know what was going on but we each did as she instructed us to do.

"I added a new business to my already successful dairy," she said.

As Annette opened the heavy door we could feel a blast of cold air that gave each one of us a chill. She took a lantern from a nail just outside the door and lit it since there were no windows inside.

We walked into the room shivering, and to a large vat-type container. Annette lifted the lid and told us, "Here taste this and see if you don't think you have died and gone to heaven."

We did, and the smooth texture that touched our lips was none other than delicious ice cream! Annette built her business on the word of God. Every morning as soon as her feet hit the floor she is praising God and thanking Him for blessing her business and everyone who comes to her farm to purchase milk, and now the newest endeavor, delicious ice cream.

130

A Little Taste of Heavenly Delight!

"It was the Holy Spirit who encouraged me to add this new business venture," Annette explained. "When the Holy Spirit spoke to me I turned around to see if someone had walked up behind me. The Holy Spirit had never spoken to me aloud before. But when I turned and no one was there, I knew that it was the voice of the Holy Spirit.

"I said, 'Speak Lord because I recognize that it's You and I will shut my mouth and listen.' The Lord started to lay out a plan for me to begin freezing different flavors of ice cream and offer it to the ranchers that come to buy milk.

"Then I took a trip to Wichita to see what was available for me to begin my new adventure. It was almost unreal how I found everything just as the Holy Spirit had outlined! Sometimes we all have trouble believing that the Holy Spirit knows what He is talking about.

"I signed for the equipment and a date for shipment was made. Then I made my way back to the dairy farm and started preparing for my new business!"

Annette was really excited to tell her father about her day and what she had learned. The first thing that her father asked to her was, "How was your first taste of heavenly delight?"

Annette, startled, blurted out, "How did you know? Did someone from Wichita call you?"

Annette's father, who was a part-time circuit rider preacher, was always in touch with the Holy

Spirit and he said that He had spoken to him at the same time that she had signed the papers.

"I hope you are not upset or disappointed that I know," he said.

Annette burst into tears and threw her arms around her father and told him, "I love you and you know that I could never be upset with you!"

It was then that she adopted the slogan: "For a little taste of heaven, try Heavenly Delight ice cream."

The Holy Spirit had told her to build her business according to Him and that He personally would see that it did not fail.

We loaded up the wagon with the milk and as you have already guessed, a bunch of her delicious Heavenly Delight ice cream.

You may be wondering how Annette can take a wagonload of ice cream sixty miles without it melting, but you see, during the cold winter months the ponds and lakes freeze over and workers saw the ice into blocks sometimes weighing as much as a hundred pounds. The ice is carried back and stored in an icehouse. This icehouse has really thick walls that are filled with sawdust from the sawmill, and the ice will last for a whole month without melting. Annette uses some of the ice to make her ice cream and then wraps it tightly in burlap cloth and places it beside the other ice blocks.

I thought that I finally had one over on Pastor Wells and I couldn't wait to tell him about Annette and her new business. When I met him at church Sunday, the first words out of his mouth were, "How was your new treat?"

I gave out an, "Oh man, He has done it again!"

You see, Annette not only knew and believed in tithing but she practiced it with all her might. This is the reason her businesses are so successful.

Annette patiently waiting for Ol' Smokey, Blake, and the Ol' Cowpoke.

Another load of Heavenly Delight ice cream!

CHAPTER 24

Sister Susan Steps in as the Wells Go Wichita Bound

*And in the same house remain, eating and drinking such
things as they give: for the labourer is worthy of his hire.
Go not from house to house.
And into whatsoever city ye enter, and they receive you,
eat such things that are set before you:
And heal the sick that are therein, and say unto them, the
kingdom of God is come nigh unto you. (KJV)*
—Luke 10:7-9

Well howdy saddle pals! It was just the other day
when Col. Dexter was having a meeting with his
staff: Ol' Smokey, manager of ranch supplies; Nancy,
general ranch manager; and me, the Ol' Cowpoke,
foreman. During this meeting, Col. Dexter told us
that we were doing such a good job and that he really
only had one thing on his mind. He told us that since
we had been blessed with Sister Susan's presence, he
felt she was a perfect substitute to fill in for Pastor
Wells for a couple of weeks. The Wells had wanted
to go for a visit to see Pastor Wells' brother and family

for a long time, and Col. Dexter thought it would be a blessing to send them on a two-week vacation to Wichita.

None of us disagreed, mainly because we knew that Col. Dexter had already made up his mind and that's that. Col. Dexter told Nancy to call Pastor Wells' home and tell them to start packing because they had tickets and reservations for the one o'clock train the next day, which was Sunday. Nancy also told them not to worry because Sister Susan would be preaching tomorrow's sermon and would preach next Sunday as well.

Sister Susan gave her remarks along the line of an outsider's observance of how much the townspeople loved and appreciated Pastor Wells and all his family. She said that even though her being a part of West Fork had been so short she had fallen in love with every thing about this small town with its friendly atmosphere. As Sister Susan referred to her text she recollected the things that she had heard about Pastor Wells and how he had become like an adopted member of everyone's family here. Sister Susan said that she didn't know how much the church was paying him, but she believed that he was worth it and more. She spoke of Scripture that the servant is worthy of his hire. She also told the congregation that the Holy Spirit is a qualified accountant and He is making note of all the times everyone has blessed Pastor Wells and his family. She also made it clear that God our heavenly Father is not indebted to anyone.

At the close of the service, Sister Susan invited everyone to come forth and extend a hand of friendship to Pastor Wells, his wife, Rachel, and their son, Jamie. Then we would all gather at the railroad station for our benediction and a grand sendoff.

The whole congregation was there to see them off.

"God bless you! We love you!" some of us shouted.

"We'll miss you! Don't be gone long!" still others shouted.

They finally had to stop with the goodbyes and board the train because the conductor was getting mighty edgy and kept looking at his watch. With a sniffle and a tear, everyone waved as the train rattled off, rounded the bend, and went out of sight.

Sister Susan stepped forward and gave a farewell wave as she lifted a prayer for a safe and refreshing trip for the Wells.

Pastor Wells and Sister Rachel, but where is Jamie?

CHAPTER 25

Ol' Higgy and the Floating Elephant

With them in the boat were pairs of every kind of animal—domestic and wild—and reptiles and birds of every sort.
Two by two they came, male and female, just as God had commanded. Then the Lord God closed the door and shut them in. (LB)
—Genesis 7:14-16

Howdy saddle pals, it's tall tale time again with your pal the Ol' Cowpoke himself. You remember, saddle pals, the time when Ol' Higgy, the blacksmith and Rosalie Delmontico gave shabbily-dressed Chester Parsons twenty-five dollars to help them sneak away on a picnic? Well while Ol' Higgy and Rosalie were sitting on the bank of the ol' James River just talking Rosalie sorta shouted out for Ol' Higgy to look yonder. He looked in the direction Rosalie was pointing and, in disbelief, saw an elephant floating down the river on a raft! The raft was approaching a thirty-foot, life-threatening waterfall!

Even though Ol' Higgy was a blacksmith he wasn't any good without his tools. He knew that it would take too long to go get them and the raft would be over the falls by the time he returned. He began to look over the landscape to see if there was something that could be used to rescue the elephant and he knew he was short on time.

As he was searching for something, Rosalie yelled out that over in the little thicket across the river was a grapevine hanging down from a tall tree. As he looked up he thought that might actually work, but it was on the other side of the river and here he was without any swimming trunks.

Suddenly Rosalie pulled a pair of swimming trunks out of her apron. She had bought them at Belle's and brought them along in case Ol' Higgy decided to go for a dip later.

Ol' Higgy walked over to a thick brush area and threw on his trunks and dove into the water. It didn't take Ol' Higgy long to swim across and he scrambled up the bank. He pulled the grapevine out so he could cut the bottom end and started pulling the vine to the edge of the water. Ol' Higgy used a rock to pound the vine in two, tied the vine around his waist, and once again jumped into the water. Ol' Higgy was shivering as he surfaced in the cold river water. He soon reached the raft and knew that he would have to work fast because the falls were mighty close.

Ol' Higgy quickly tied the vine to the rear of the raft and it stretched at the weight of the elephant and raft but it held tight. The flow of the current caused the raft to swing toward the bank and the elephant lumbered onto dry ground.

As the big animal was disappearing into the woods, Ol' Higgy jumped off the raft and untied the end of the vine sending it cascading over the falls.

When Ol' Higgy and Rosalie got back to Delmonty's where they had left Chester, they sat down and started telling him about their adventure. That's just when I had come in and found that the Lord had indeed kept them safe all this time I was out looking for them.

I had left Spirit the Wonder Horse at Ol' Higgy's blacksmith shop for some new shoes. Ol' Higgy stayed late just to do the shoeing of Spirit's feet. I called back to the Delta D to let Col. Dexter know where I was but that I would need to stay in town for the night. I also called Jane, my wife, to let her know too.

I learned from Nancy that Col. Dexter was not at home. He had come by just long enough to shower and shave and had returned to West Fork because he and Sister Susan were going on a missionary trip that would take them away for a couple of weeks. He said as he walked out the door that he had an announcement to make when he returned.

The next day with Spirit sporting a brand new set of shoes, he and I rode down to the river where Ol' Higgy and Rosalie had seen the elephant disappear into the woods. I traveled quite a distance but I saw no sign of the elephant. To this day there has been no sight or sound of such an elephant.

That night we went with Chester to the train station and watched as he disappeared into the night. As he was shaking hands with me he put a twenty-dollar bill and a five-dollar bill into my hand and told me that after he had left to give it to Ol' Higgy and Rosalie and tell them that the experience was more than enough payment for what little bit he had done. He told me that he didn't need the money, that he was a millionaire and was going back to Wichita to once again take his place on his farm. He said that West Fork was too wild for him.

You saddle pals wonder if the Holy Spirit had prompted Rosalie to buy the trunks or do you suppose that He might have put them in a place where she would see and buy them?

After we had relayed the story to Pastor Wells his only comment was, "I know. I have already heard from the Holy Spirit and just you wait until Sunday for the rest of the story."

Pastor Wells told us that God had a purpose for the elephant turning up at just that time and we may never know the complete story until we all get to heaven where we can sit down with Jesus and have Him tell us the rest of the story.

W. Odell Mann

Without his shotgun, he don't look like no outlaw!

The ol' vine just hanging 'round.

CHAPTER 26

Over the Rise with the Ol' Cowpoke and Doc Jenni

All kinds of fruit trees will grow along the river banks. The leaves will never turn brown and fall, and there will always be fruit. There will be a new crop every month—without fail! For they are watered by the river flowing from the Temple. The fruit will be for food and the leaves for medicine. (LB)
—Ezekial 48:12

All of us cowboys, twenty-six in number, had already bedded down for the night and just when I was about to drop off to sleep I thought I could hear a wagon rolling up. The campfire was nothing but smoke by now so there was no way to see what might be approaching. I knew that the sound was a wagon so I rolled back my blanket and went to the smoldering fire. I stirred the embers and pretty soon the blaze arose. I could not see the approaching wagon because the night was as pitch dark as tar. There was not a star in sight, nor was the moon illuminating the sky.

As I peered into the blackness of the night I thought that I could see a faint glow just over the rise about a hundred feet or so away. The sound of the wagon wheels rolling on the rocky ground got louder and louder as it approached. By now I became a little unnerved so I woke all the other drovers and we hurried to the cattle because we all knew that cattle don't like strange noises in the night. The herd had started to get nervous and fidgety and the last thing we needed was a stampede in the middle of the night.

One of the rowdies grabbed his guitar and started to pick out a tune and all the others started to hum a gentle melody and the herd began to settle down a bit. By now the faint glow had become brighter and we could tell that it was a lantern swinging on the side of a wagon. We continued to hum along as three or four cowboys started toward the wagon. We knew that any sudden move from the wagon could cause the cattle to spook. Suddenly, by the light of the lantern, we saw sitting on the seat a young lady. She looked to be in her late twenties or early thirties and dressed in a white coat that looked like one of Doc Percy's lab coats. I jumped up onto the seat beside the young lady and eased the wagon up to the campfire. To my surprise, this beautiful lady leaned her head over onto my shoulder and was sound asleep in a matter of seconds. She must have traveled all day and into the night and was just plain tuckered out. I guided the team up to the fire and jumped down and lifted the lady off the seat and carried her to a blanket one of the cowboys had spread out next to the campfire.

As I laid this sleeping beauty on the blanket, the light from the fire shined on her glowing cheeks. Her beauty illuminated the camp. I covered her up and she seemed to nestle down into the folds of the blanket much like a baby.

I believe the Holy Spirit had already let her know that she was in no danger and that she had no need to be afraid. We learned later that this gorgeous young lady was in fact a born-again, spirit-filled, Bible-toting, Jesus-proclaiming Christian.

The next morning after everyone had got out of his bedroll and got everything ready to start the herd moving, we woke up our guest. She said that she had slept so hard that every bone in her body was aching and that she needed to walk a little while to limber up. I said that would be fine but for her to take the guitar and strum every once in a while to let us know that she was still all right. When she returned we asked her name.

"Jennifer Savage," she said, "but you can call me Jenni. I'm a doctor and I came to Kansas looking for a particular herb that I use in a preparation for relieving arthritis. I understand this herb can only be found in this region."

After breakfast Jenni took a bucket off the chuck wagon and said that she was going to walk just over the rise a short ways and see if there were any of the herbs that she was searching for. She thought that she recognized one of the plants in the faint glimmer of the lantern as she rode along the night before. I asked if I could join her and she sounded like she would appreciate the company.

We were only gone for a little while when she said it was just a wild goose chase anyway and that the plant was just a cactus and of no value.

When we got back to camp we helped Jenni water her team and get on board her wagon. Then we were on our way again.

About three o'clock we rolled into the ranch and stabled our horses and put Jenni's team into stalls and gave them water and grain. Of course Spirit was expecting his usual sugar lump!

After we had finished tending the stock, Jenni and I walked over to the Big House. I wanted Jenni to meet Nancy, knowing they would become good friends. The guys had already fallen in love with Jenni and we couldn't wait for Nancy to meet her. I told Nancy how we came to meet Jennifer and thought that it would be a good idea for us to take her to West Fork the next day to meet Doc Percy. This would be right down his alley. Doc Percy is always messing around with special herbs and spices. Why, just the other day he asked me to try something he had mixed that would cure the hiccups.

Jenni was up bright and early the next morning, excited as ever to go to town and meet Doc Percy. Nancy had called Doc Percy's office and told him she was bringing someone to his office that he would like to meet.

When Nancy and Jenni got to the office, Doc Percy was standing on the porch and walked out to meet them. After Nancy had introduced Jenni to Doc Percy she told them that she had some shopping to do and that she would be back in a couple of hours.

Meanwhile, Jenni showed Doc Percy her wagon, which was her make-shift laboratory. By the time Nancy returned, it was getting close to eating time so the three of them walked over to Delmonty's for lunch. Rosalie cooked up her special, rattlesnake stew. Jenni said that she had never tasted snake stew before but she was game to try anything at least once. As the three of them sat and ate, Doc Percy and Jenni exchanged their medical research findings. We could tell there was a mutual interest that would lead to a smooth relationship taking place.

Doc Percy and Nancy took Jenni and walked over to the church to let her meet Pastor Wells.

Sunday morning Pastor Wells told the congregation that he wanted them to meet a special person that was staying at the Delta D Ranch. Her name, as he continued, was Doctor Jennifer Savage and that she would probably be working some with our own Doc Percy.

Pastor Wells explained to us that God has given to us His creation, all sorts of plants and herbs that are for the making of medicines for our ills.

You see, our Lord and Savior is always interested in our well-being.

*"Say 'ah' and cough,"
says Doc Savage to
one of Doc Percy's
patients.*

*The picture of
health. "That little
heart is perfect,"
says Doc Jenni.*

CHAPTER 27

The Ol' Cowpoke Meets Carmen del Rio

*How we praise God, the Father of our Lord Jesus
Christ, who has blessed us with every blessing in
Heaven because we belong to Christ. (LB)*
—Ephesians 1:3

Ya know, saddle pals, we never know what we will
find each time we are driving cattle back toward the
Delta D Ranch. This one time even I, the Ol' Cow-
poke, was surprised and really quite shocked! We
were driving the two thousand head of cattle from
about three hundred miles to the ranch. Col. Dexter
had bought this herd while he and Sister Susan were
on a revival trip to a small village on the Kansas bor-
der. When Col. Dexter met Sister Susan it was love at
first sight. To be around the two of them you would
have thought that they were love struck teenagers. It
was a joy to behold the difference in Col. Dexter's
behavior. You see, he could never really accept his
wife's death. He kept blaming himself for not being
with her when she died. He always believed that if
he had not been on a cattle-buying trip but with her,

that he could have done something to keep her from leaving him—as he put it. Even though he knew in his heart that she had the best of care and that everything that could be done was done for her. Now that he has met Sister Susan he has become alive again and it is absolutely super to see the change in his life. Col. Dexter has now become heavily involved in Sister Susan's ministry and has rented a place in town that is large enough for her to live in and have an office for her ministerial business and supplies.

Col. Dexter has now become engaged to Sister Susan and there will soon be a wedding date set.

They came to this little village by accident. Col. Dexter and Sister Susan had taken the train from West Fork to a town north of the Kansas border. About fifty miles from the border the train experienced some mechanical difficulty and they were told that it would be about twenty hours or so before the train would be repaired and be on its way again. Col. Dexter is not one for sitting around for a long period of time. He gets restless and grumpy. One of his favorite expressions that we drovers often hear is, "An hour lost is two hours wasted."

When the conductor told them that it would be a while, Col. Dexter started to get in one of his moods again. He always carried Sally, his faithful steed, with him even when he traveled by train. The train had cars just for the horses of the passengers. Along with Sally, they had brought along Sister Susan's beautiful palomino mare, Blondie, that Col. Dexter had given to her as an engagement gift.

Col. Dexter asked the conductor to drop the gangplank so they could take Sally and Blondie off the train and ride a ways while they were waiting for the repairs. They mounted their horses and lit out to see what lay on the other side of the hill. They had ridden about three hours when all of a sudden they could see what looked like a small town in the wide open spaces many miles from anywhere. They stepped up their pace and pretty soon had entered the quaint little town. As they rode down the only street they began to notice the businesses along the way. The first was the livery stable with a blacksmith shop adjoining. Next door to the livery stable was a small bank attended by a single teller but no customers. Next door to the bank was an interesting looking restaurant with only one person inside. Col. Dexter and Sister Susan were so intrigued by the little restaurant with no diners that they dismounted and went inside. The lady graciously greeted them and led them to a table right in the center of the room. Col. Dexter pulled out the chair like a perfect gentleman and assisted Sister Susan to her seat. Col. Dexter seated himself across the table. The lady was not only the owner and cook but also the server as well.

She handed them the tastefully designed, handwritten menu and they were soon served the most mouth-watering food they had ever tasted.

Since it was pretty evident that the place was not busy, the lady came over with a cup of coffee and asked if she could sit down with them. She introduced herself as Carmen del Rio and told them that she had inherited this restaurant from her father who had founded this town about fifty years before. He had built the town from scratch and had run the whole town up until two weeks prior when he suddenly died from some mysterious, peculiar illness. Miss del Rio told them that she had not left town because she was hoping that the town would spring up again and be like it was before. She said that she felt she owed it to the memory of her father to at least wait as long as she could. Miss del Rio told them that she believed that the time had come for her to pack up and go somewhere to begin her life anew.

Col. Dexter right away bellowed out, "Ain't that just like Jesus? Here I have been praying for the Holy Spirit to help me find someone to be Nancy's assistant back at the ranch and here in this uncharted place is the answer to my prayer."

Col. Dexter wasted no time telling Carmen about the Delta D and all the things that were going on around there.

"Carmen, would you consider coming to West Fork to join the gang at the Delta D?" he asked.

Carmen told him that she believed in the divine guidance of the Holy Spirit and she believed that He had within His will used this train mishap to bring this opportunity into her life. Carmen wasted no time packing her clothes and putting them in her covered wagon that had been in the family for as long as she could remember. Carmen told Col. Dexter that just over the rise were two thousand head of cattle that had belonged to her father and she would make him a super deal if he would take the whole herd. Here again, was the moving of the Holy Spirit because Col. Dexter was keeping his eyes open while he was on this trip for an opportunity to buy some cattle. Col. Dexter felt that it was the leading of the Holy Spirit that he and Sister Susan should accompany Carmen back to the ranch.

They all went back to the train and picked up their luggage and tied Blondie to the back of the wagon. Col. Dexter told the conductor their plans had changed and to go on without them. He also told the conductor to telegraph me, the Ol' Cowpoke, from the next town and tell me where I could meet up with them and the new herd.

It took three weeks to return the cattle to the ranch and Col. Dexter, Sister Susan, and Miss del Rio had been back about two weeks when we finally arrived. This was a long, tedious cattle drive. I think that Col. Dexter was dreading the first time that Nancy saw Carmen because this was not the usual way of doing things at the ranch. It was a policy that anytime a person was to be considered for hiring, they would be introduced to everyone before anything was said about a possible position on the ranch.

Col. Dexter had already made up his mind about hiring Miss del Rio way back at the border.

Would you believe that the Holy Spirit had already prepared Nancy's spirit and she was as calm as could be. Why do we mortals get so uptight and think that the Holy Spirit doesn't know what He is doing and that He is never caught by surprise?

Miss del Rio fit in from the start and quickly became one of the gang. The way that Nancy and Carmen took to each other you would have thought they were long-lost sisters. Nancy was now able to put her full attention on the duties that her new position demanded. She had been promoted to full manager of the Big House and of all the employees that Col. Dexter managed, except the cowboys.

Ol' Smokey also was delighted at meeting Carmen and some said that they could detect a sparkle in his eye when they first were introduced. We'll have to wait and see about that, won't we?

As usual, Pastor Wells had prepared his message for Sunday with uncanny accuracy. Matter of fact his first words from the pulpit were, "Praise God from whom all blessings flow."

Pastor Wells was his usual self as he delivered the message that the Holy Spirit had given him to bless us with and as usual tears were flowing all across the congregation. At the invitation for salvation, a young couple that had been coming for some time stood and asked Pastor Wells if they could come forward and speak to the folks. Pastor Wells responded with the affirmative.

The young couple made an announcement that they believed that God was calling them to a full time ministry as a missionary to a tribe of Indians that they had heard needed Divine guidance. Pastor Wells asked the congregation to come down and gather around the young couple and lay hands on them and send them off with all our blessings. Someone made a motion from the crowd that this tribe be added to our missionary support by our funding. Pastor Wells called for a second and a vote. Of course the vote was unanimous in the affirmative and everyone left with a cheer and a song as they walked out.

Carmen sez goodbye to ol' Ironsides the wood stove.

CHAPTER 28

The Ol' Cowpoke Picks
Up a Book at Jeanne's

*Study to shew thyself approved unto God, a
workman that needeth not to be ashamed,
rightly dividing the word of truth. (KJV)*
—Timothy 2:15

Rosalie's boarding house, Delmonty's, has become
one of Jane's and my favorite places, which is where
she and I found ourselves just the other day. You see,
saddle pals, we were just sitting there having lunch
after a long day of shopping. I believe Jane was the
one who coined the saying "Shop til I drop." She
drags me on one of her shopping trips until I am the
one who drops! Anyway, as we were eating I hap-
pened to notice a lady sitting across the room that I
could tell was real nervous. She kept glancing toward
the door as if she was expecting someone that she
wasn't looking forward to seeing. Every few minutes
she would get up and walk over to the window and
look both up and down the street and then go back to
her chair and sit down.

I looked over at Jane and told her to watch this lady across the room.

Jane asked, kinda agitated, "What am I supposed to be looking for?"

I told her to watch because the lady looked like she was scared about something.

I decided that Jane and I would walk over to the lady's table and see if there was anything we could do. You see, being the shy, bashful type, I find it kinda hard to meet people, but Jane said that she would protect me, so we started toward her table. Just as we got part of the way, two men came in the door, stopped, and scanned the room. It was pretty obvious that they were looking for someone.

We continued on across the room and we stood with the lady between us. You could tell that these two men were some kind of official people because of the way they were dressed. The lady really became nervous and we could tell that she knew who the two men were. The men saw this lady and started toward her table. I stepped in front of her and started to speak to the men to try to find out why the lady was so frightened of them. One of the men very abruptly spoke to me in a manner that let me know that any questions from me were not needed nor were they wanted.

"Now look here, Sir, whoever you are," I said, "you can't come in here and frighten this young lady and I believe you just better leave or I will go and get Sheriff Ben and you'll be sorry."

"Ha!" he replied. "Go on and get the sheriff and then we'll see who'll be sorry."

"Ok," I said, "let's start over again and be a little more civilized. I'm called the Ol' Cowpoke, and you see sirs, we here in West Fork sorta feel that visitors who come here should feel welcomed and protected from the harassment of someone who just out of the blue yonder wanders in and starts throwing his weight around. Will you grant me the privilege of inviting you two gentlemen to sit down and have a cup of Rosalie's coffee and chat? "

The men sat down with us.

"As I said, I am the Cowpoke, the foreman at the Delta D Ranch just a few miles west of here. This here's my wife, Jane, and we come in here real regularly to eat and fellowship with those who have come in to do likewise. We see this nervous lady here, then suddenly you two come bustin' through the door. Now I would like to know who you two are."

One of the men jumped into the conversation before the lady could speak and very angrily said, "I'll tell you who she is and—"

"Hold it mister," I said sharpy. "You'll get your turn. Let me hear what this lady has to say first."

We all waited for the lady to speak.

"My name is Jeanne Bartholomew. I just got off the train to exercise my legs and to see if there was a friendly face somewhere about. Now I don't really know what these men are all about but I have an idea that it has something to do with the book that I have in this carpetbag I'm carrying."

The bag looked like it had weathered a lot of storms. Jeanne opened the tattered bag and brought out a big book that must have weighed thirty pounds or more. She laid the book on the table and I saw that there was an inscription on the cover that read Holy Bible. Now I will admit that I was getting very interested.

One of the men interrupted and yelled out, "Yeah, she stole it from my boss and we have been chasing her all the way from New York City."

I held up my hand to stop the man from continuing and told Jeanne to go ahead.

"I did not steal the book. I bought it from a man back in New York City. He told me that it was his inheritance and it was quite valuable. He told me it was a reproduction of the famous Gutenberg Bible and that he would not part with the book except that he needed the money. He told me he could sell it for about twenty thousand dollars, but that he needed to get to California in a week because there was a job waiting for him there. He told me I could have the book for a thousand dollars if I would take it right then." Jeanne started to cry. "I had been saving money to go to Wichita to meet my father and we were going on to Yuma, Arizona.

"All I had in the world was a thousand dollars and train fare to Wichita. Foolishly I gave the man the money and he handed me the bag with the book in it. I was having a cup of coffee in a little diner in New York City when I happened to glance at a piece of paper that had been tacked to the wall. On the paper were these words written in big letters. 'Reward for information leading to the capture of the persons who stole a valuable reproduction of the Gutenberg Bible.' There was a telephone number on the paper and I went and called to try to find out something about the reward. The man who answered asked where he could meet me and I told him that I would be at the train station in about an hour because I was going to Wichita as soon as I had the reward money.

"Sure enough the two men that you see here were the ones who met me. I asked about the reward and someone there told me that there was no reward and that I was going to be arrested for stealing the book. I started to run as fast as I could which was not very fast because of the weight of the bag. I screamed that these men were chasing me and that they were going to kill me. Then out of nowhere a couple of men jumped on these men and wrestled them to the ground and an officer held a gun on them and told me that they would hold them until I had boarded the train and it had pulled away. As I was sitting down on the train I could see out the window the men were showing their badges and they were released. They started toward the train. The train started to move and I lost sight of them. As we were pulling into the station at West Fork and I was getting off, I thought that I spotted the men and I ran in here hoping that they had not seen me."

In between sobs Jeanne said that she feared she would be arrested and put into jail. I assured her that she would not be going to jail until I find out more. During this time Jane had gone to find Sheriff Ben. I was turning to the men and was saying that it was their time to tell their side of the story when Jane and Sheriff Ben came in and sat down at our table. One of the men spoke up and introduced himself as Boyd Lesley and he and his partner Burle Watson were trying to question this lady about a stolen article that she had in the carpetbag. He said they were special detectives hired by the museum in New York City to track down the thief or thieves who took this valuable book and fled.

Sheriff Ben likes to throw his weight around and every time he gets a chance to sound rough and with great authority he does so. You see, nothing ever happens in this law-abiding town that needs the hand of the law to butt in. This time, however, Sheriff Ben really started in on the men and fired off questions faster than they could think up an answer. He asked them the telephone number for the museum that had hired them. The men kinda stuttered around and Sheriff Ben said, "I didn't think you knew and I believe that you two are going to spend some time in my jail until I can find out what the true story is."

"Why don't we forget about the whole thing, huh?" Burle said.

Sheriff Ben told them that since there would not be another train before the next morning and since they had no place to stay he believed they should be the guests of the town and spend the night in jail.

I never miss a chance to witness for the Lord Jesus Christ so I told the two men that Jesus loved them and He wanted to become their savior and now was the accepted day of salvation.

Burle spoke up and said to Sheriff Ben, "Take us to jail sheriff, we don't want to hear no preaching from no farm boy."

Well I tried and a seed was sown. Now it's up to the Holy Spirit to do the growing.

Just as Sheriff Ben was escorting Burle and Boyd off to jail, in walked none other than Col. Dexter and Sister Susan. He had seen Jane's and my buckboard outside at the hitching rail and thought they would stop in and see how things were going at the ranch.

You remember how Col. Dexter told me that Sister Susan and he had an announcement to make when they returned from their ministry trip? I believe that this was the real reason that they stopped in because he couldn't wait any longer to spread the news. Col. Dexter knew that to tell me was like having it in big letters in *The Fork Over Gazette*. I felt in my spirit that I already knew what the colonel was going to say. Col. Dexter turned to me and winked and then announced that Sister Susan had agreed to be his wife. Their wedding date was to be in two months on October third. He added that things were going to be a little hectic around West Fork and the Delta D for the next few weeks.

Col. Dexter asked what all the excitement was about because he saw Sheriff Ben taking the two men to jail. I asked him to sit down and I introduced him and Sister Susan to Jeanne and I told them about her ordeal.

Jeanne took the book out of the bag and told the brief story of how she had become the owner of a very valuable reproduction of the famous Gutenberg Bible. Sister Susan spoke up that she had the pleasure of seeing the original Bible in a museum about five years ago. She told us that this book did not even resemble the original and that it was a possibility that it was a fake and not worth much. At this Jeanne's heart was broken and she began to cry again and said that she didn't know what she would do because she didn't have any money left.

Col. Dexter said, "This is almost unbelievable but I think that I see the hand of our heavenly Father just itching to bless one of His children."

I had already asked Jeanne if she was a Christian and she blurted out, "You bet your ever-loving life I am." Col. Dexter told us that just the other day he and Sister Susan had felt in their spirit that West Fork needed a Christian bookstore and they were considering just such a venture. The only problem was that there was no one to take care of and manage the store since Sister Susan's ministry took up all her time.

I looked over at Jeanne and asked if she had ever worked in a bookstore. Her answer almost floored me. She replied, "I have been a librarian for all my adult life and was responsible for all the operations and purchasing of every book in a giant library in New York City."

I was overwhelmed and hollered out, "Praise the name of Jesus!" That is when The Family Book Store was born. Col. Dexter footed the entire expense for Sister Susan and Jeanne to open their own bookstore and become partners. Sister Susan wouldn't spend much time in the operation of the store but she felt confident that Jeanne, with the leadership of the Holy Spirit, would do fine.

Jane and I ran up to the church where we knew that Pastor Wells would be reviewing his Sunday sermon. We thought that surely he didn't know anything about the new addition to the town. Would you believe that the first thing Pastor Wells said when we walked in was, "I want to buy a copy of *In His Steps*. Hurry up and get it." We couldn't believe what we were hearing! The Holy Spirit had beaten us to the punch again and gone and told Pastor Wells the whole story. Oh well, He knows what is best and He is always having fun with us and we love His sense of humor.

Sunday morning the whole church was brimming with excitement and could not wait to hear what the Holy Spirit had dropped in Pastor Wells' spirit to share with us through his sermon.

Pastor Wells included in his remarks that a Christian bookstore would be a welcomed addition to West Fork and that he would greatly encourage everyone to visit the store regularly so that the Holy Spirit could inspire and uplift all of us as we read and study His word.

Oh, by the way, Jeanne has the address of the man who sold her the book and she is keeping in touch with him regularly out in California. Jeanne also told us that she had written to her father in Wichita and that he is coming to West Fork. I believe I see another story fixing to happen.

The book about Jesus.

W. Odell Mann

*Jeanne sez "Just come on in
and browse" at Jeanne's Bookstore.*

CHAPTER 29

The Ol' Cowpoke Sez "Come to the Big House"

Peter therefore was kept in prison: but prayer was made
without ceasing of the church unto God for him.
And when he had considered the thing, he came to the
house of Mary the mother of John, whose surname was
Mark; where many were gathered together praying.
And as Peter knocked at the door of the gate,
a damsel came to hearken, named Rhoda.
And when she knew Peter's voice, she opened not the gate
for gladness, but ran in, and told how
Peter stood before the gate.
And they said unto her, Thou art mad.
But she constantly affirmed that it was even so.
Then said they, it is his angel.
But Peter continued knocking: and when they had opened
the door, and saw him, they were astonished. (KJV)
—Acts 12:5, 12-16

Well howdy saddle pals! I'm just enjoying a nice glass of milk out here on the porch of the Big House. You know, I don't believe I've told you the story of our wonderful Big House at the Delta D. Allow me—

Way back in 1876, Col. Dexter's great grandfather, Baxtel Dexter (known as Mr. D), built a huge house for his bride, Leona Springer. The reason that Mr. D built such a large and magnificent structure was because Leona was an only child and she requested a giant house to be built so she could have a large family. It took about a year to complete the house and all this time Leona was getting everything in order because Mr. D had asked her to marry him and she had accepted his proposal with great enthusiasm. One of the reasons that Mr. D had settled on this place was that there was a giant grapevine just a few hundred yards from the house and Leona just fell in love with this vine from the first time she laid eyes on it. There was something about that grapevine that made her think that she had to have it.

Mr. D met the owner Lester McFadden, who showed him the land layout that he had sketched and started to tell him all about the land. Mr. D said that he didn't care about the details except how much land he could get and if the grapevine was on the property.

Lester told him that the tract of land surrounding the giant grapevine was one thousand and one acres. Lester said that also on this land was the best spring water ever found in this part of the country. Lester told Mr. D that there was a ten-acre pond exactly a half-mile behind the grapevine that had a ten-pound bass just begging to be caught. Mr. D told

Lester that he didn't care about that, just the grape-vine and how soon he could get the deed.

Since today was Saturday, Lester asked if Monday was soon enough that the land office over in Wichita would be open. Mr. D agreed to wait that long. He had built up quite a passel of money and paid cash for the giant piece of property. No one ever knew where Mr. D kept his money all those years because he didn't trust banks.

That evening when Mr. D went to court Miss Leona, he told her what he had bought and she fainted upon hearing the news. When Leona fell to the floor her father heard the crash. He didn't like Mr. D. Mr. Springer called him Ol' Brown Britches. Well, this didn't matter to Mr. D nor Miss Leona because they kept right on planning their wedding. On their wedding day the last piece of furniture was put in place in the house that was to be later called the Big House.

On February 3, 1877, Mr. Baxtel James Dexter wed Miss Leona Mason Springer and carried her over the threshold to start their family. This union led the eventual appearance of Col. James Garfield Dexter.

For the next eighteen years a new little Dexter invaded the home of Baxtel and Leona every three years. James (Col. Dexter) was the youngest. He was born in 1895. That year brought the joy of their son but also one tragedy after another. One day Mr. Dexter came home from Wichita and found Leona lying on the floor. She had been beaten within an inch of her life. Mr. D, after attending to his wife, started to look for the children because he had not seen any of them since he had come into the house. As he called out he thought that he heard a noise coming from the kitchen. Mr. D opened the kitchen door but he didn't see anyone. He was about to turn and walk away when he heard a sound coming from the pantry. Mr. D made his way across the room and unlocked the pantry door. Leona always kept the pantry door locked because she didn't want the children to pull cans off the shelves and hurt themselves. Mr. D couldn't believe his eyes. There on the floor bound and gagged were three-year-old Grace, six-year-old Bonita, nine-year-old Wesley, twelve-year-old twins Benjamin and Donald, and fifteen-year-old Warren. There was no sign of little James (Col. Dexter) anywhere. Upon questioning Warren, Mr. Dexter learned that two men with shotguns had entered the house, beaten Leona, and left her for dead. They had tied and gagged the children and locked them in the pantry. The key to the pantry door was always kept hanging above the door out of reach of the children. Warren, the oldest, told Mr. Dexter that the second man had picked up James and said for us to tell our father that this would be the last time that we would ever see James alive again.

Naturally Mr. D was devastated but even back then everyone had great faith. Mr. D visited all the neighbors for miles around and pleaded for them to start a prayer vigil. It was amazing that people started piling in and dropping to their knees and began praying for the safety of little James. About three the following morning, Pastor Whitley, the circuit rider preacher, came riding up on his horse, dismounted and knocked on the door.

Someone went and answered the door. They slammed the door in his face to run back inside and holler out that Pastor Whitley was at the door with Baby James in his arms. Everyone was praying so intently that they didn't hear the announcement. She repeated that Pastor Whitley was at the door. This time they heard and ran to the door where Pastor Whitley was still standing outside, holding James, wondering what was wrong with those people.

Pastor Whitley told all the folks that the two men had been captured and little James had been rescued and was unharmed. Everyone then fell on their knees and started praying again. This time, however, the prayers were in thanksgiving to our heavenly Father for hearing their prayers.

After the dust had settled and the kidnapping trial was over, the two men who kidnapped little James were sentenced to fifty years in jail. Mr. D visited the two men in prison because he wanted to find out the reason they kidnapped James. The trial never did make this clear. It turned out that they had made a mistake. James was not the one the men were after. To show you what kind of man Mr. D was he told them that they were forgiven and led them both to accept Jesus as their Savior. Mr. D even hired a lawyer to try and open their case for a new trial.

In June of 1906, tragedy struck again. The entire house was destroyed by fire. Fortunately, everyone had gotten out safely. Mr. D began rebuilding immediately and is the house we call the Big House.

Pastor Wells, Sister Rachel, and son Jamie were having dinner with Jane and me at our house when I told this story to them. Pastor Wells said that this reminded him of a similar occasion when Peter was in jail and the ladies were praying for his release.

Author's Note:

Since the stories in the book *The Ol' Cowpoke Sez Howdy* are fictional there needs to be a clarifying account of the house that is called the Big House.

In Fayetteville, North Carolina, there stands a beautiful house called Poe House. The Poe House is a most interesting segment of the Museum of the Cape Fear Historical Complex, a part of the Division of North Carolina History Museums within the North Carolina Department of Cultural Resources. After visiting the Poe House, the writer thought that this was the perfect place to be depicted for these stories. Anyone viewing the Poe House will right away be struck with the beauty and integrity that abounds. The Poe House has been restored in its original stately grandeur and stands as a reminder of how much we have strayed from the majestic, spellbinding beauty of our heritage. As you, the reader, take the time to give a glance at the Poe House as illustrated in this book, may you, too, long for the high quality of the olden days.

The ol' Big House is our mansion on a hilltop.

CHAPTER 30

Col. Dexter and Sister Susan Come Across a Little Nameless Town

For I was an hungered, and ye gave me meat; I was thirsty, and ye gave me drink; I was a stranger, and ye took me in; naked, and ye clothed me; I was sick, and ye visited me; I was in prison, and ye came unto me.
Then shall the righteous answer him, saying, Lord, when saw we thee an hungered, and fed thee? Or thirsty, and gave thee drink? When saw we thee a stranger, and took thee in? Or naked, and clothed thee? Or when saw we thee sick? Or in prison, and came unto thee? And the King shall answer and say unto them, Verily I say unto you, in as much as ye have done it unto one of the least of these my brethren, ye have done it unto Me. (KJV)
—Matthew 25:35-40

Howdy saddle pals! You won't believe it but Col. Dexter and Sister Susan have become engaged and Col. Dexter was like a little boy at Christmas time, always so happy around the ranch. The staff and ranch hands just couldn't believe their eyes when they saw Col. Dexter bouncing around like a newborn calf.

Well saddle pals, Col. Dexter and Sister Susan were on one of their trips to Nebraska. They were going there to find Great Katherine who was crusading through the Midwest. They were taking the train this trip and were just inside the Nebraska and South Dakota border when the train stopped to take on water.

Col. Dexter looked out the window and couldn't believe his eyes. He called Sister Susan over to the window and asked her what she saw. Sister Susan looked out and said that she couldn't see anything. She quizzed him about what she was supposed to see. Col. Dexter said that was exactly what he was talking about. The little community was waist deep in weeds and the few people that he could see looked like they had not eaten in days. Col. Dexter told Sister Susan that he had to see just what was going on here.

Col. Dexter always takes their horses with them when they take a trip by train because they usually leave the train and ride out to look at the countryside. The conductor dropped the gangplank and both Sally and Blondie almost jumped over the ramp in anticipation. They, too, enjoyed taking side trips and they knew that it was time to go exploring. The Col. and Sister Susan mounted and started toward the center of town as the horses waded through the deep weeds. As they trotted along they noticed that no one was talking, everyone had their head down as if they had lost their last friend. Col. Dexter couldn't stand it any longer so as they approached a young couple, he jumped down out of the saddle and assisted Sister Susan to the ground. The couple didn't seem to be interested in meeting anyone but Col. Dexter wouldn't take no for an answer. That was his style. Col. Dexter asked the couple their names and they responded that they were the Browns who lived just down the street a ways. (The street was more of a jungle than a street.) Col. Dexter asked if they could accompany them to their house and have a cup of coffee with them.

Dave, the husband, and Brenda, the wife, sorta laughed. "It's been so long since we've had a cup of coffee that we've forgotten what it tastes like!"

Col. Dexter looked at Sister Susan with a look of disbelief.

"What do you mean?" Sister Susan asked.

Sounding like he was in the depths of depression, Dave said, "Look around. There's nothing in this town but weeds and poverty. The last mouthful of food has just been eaten and nothing is left."

"Why haven't you sought help?" Col. Dexter asked.

"Some feller stopped by about three weeks ago and promised us he would go and buy some supplies if we gave him some money. So, I, being the town spokesman, held a meeting for all the townspeople. Twenty-seven people, including newborn twins from the Newby family, attended. I told the residents that this feller, Jack Nimble, would go and get food and supplies for five hundred dollars. Turned out all we could scrape together was four hundred thirteen dollars and twenty-four cents."

Brenda began to cry. "It was everything that our town had and there was nothing left!"

"What happened?" Sister Susan asked.

"The feller had no intention of returning since it's already been three weeks and no word of him," Dave explained.

Col. Dexter could not believe what he was hearing.

"Haven't you asked someone on the train to get word to the sheriff about seeing if there was something that could be done about finding the fellow that stole your money?" Col. Dexter asked.

"We tried that about a week ago but it seems that he's disappeared into thin air," Dave said. "We've accepted the fact that we were naive to trust a stranger with our savings and that we should have known better."

"What are you going to do?" Sister Susan asked. "Is there anything we can do for your town?"

"I don't know of anything except going back to the county seat to see if anything has turned up about our money," Dave said. "There just ain't much to look forward to. Starvation is inevitable."

Now Col. James Dexter was not one to accept defeat and just lie down and die because he believed that where there was life there was hope. He was one who had made the statement many times that the darkest is just before the dawn. Col. Dexter shook hands with Dave and Brenda and told them to hang tough and let him have a try at doing something for them. Col. Dexter asked if he and Sister Susan could have a prayer with them and ask the Holy Spirit to open a way for some relief in this crisis. Dave nodded, even though it looked like he had lost all hope.

Col. Dexter and Sister Susan joined hands with Dave and Brenda, leading them to kneel right there in the weeds that reached over their heads as they kneeled. Col. Dexter prayed a simple but powerful prayer of intercession on behalf of the little town amongst the wilderness.

"Holy Father, You know the situation with some of your children," he prayed. "You have seen them in their time of distress and in deep despair. We ask You right now to come into the situation and cause a turnaround in the lives of these people."

As Col. Dexter and Sister Susan mounted their horses and with one last remark to Dave and Brenda, he said, "Raise your hands in thanksgiving to the heavenly Father for answering your prayer and that to look for the answer in coming days."

Dave and Brenda raised their hands and for the first time in many days a faint smile crossed their lips.

Col. Dexter turned to Sister Susan and said, "They did not lose hope, they just needed someone to remind them that there was a way out. It is in the

Lord Jesus Christ, and the Holy Spirit has already started working in their behalf.

"Amen," Sister Susan commented.

The Col. and Sister Susan went back to the nearest town and telegraphed Pastor Wells and told him of the situation that they had just witnessed. Col. Dexter didn't waste any words or kill any time trying to decide what to do, but went straight to the problem at hand. The Col. told Pastor Wells to call the ranch and talk directly to me, the Ol' Cowpoke, to tell me what to do.

Col. Dexter told me to get five buckboards and drivers and to tell Blake to get the chuck wagon loaded with supplies for a two-week trip up to Nebraska. Ol' Smokey can fill in for him while he is gone. Now Ol' Smokey knew Col. Dexter well enough that none of this would be questioned. He instructed me to go to the general store in West Fork and fill the buckboards with all the food and supplies they will hold and set off in a wagon train north for a town called Spencer, Nebraska. He said that Sister Susan and he would meet me their in two weeks from today. Once there, they would accompany me to a small town near the South Dakota border. Col. Dexter knew that his wishes would be followed to the letter.

The next day, in the town of Spencer Col. Dexter went to the livery stable and rented a buckboard and hired a driver and went with him to the dry goods store and loaded the wagon with all the nonperishable supplies that it would hold. Col. Dexter, Sister Susan, and the wagon set out for the little town in northern Nebraska.

Would you believe that the Holy Spirit was already way ahead of the situation and just a few miles out of Spencer they came upon a large herd of sheep. Now these sheep were not at this place when Col. Dexter and Sister Susan had come by just a couple of days earlier. Ain't that just like the Holy Spirit? He's never taken by surprise.

Col. Dexter found the trail boss and was told that he could find the owner of the sheep at the head of the herd. Col. Dexter and Sister Susan coaxed Sally and Blondie into a gallop and soon were alongside Warner Benton, the sheep's owner.

Col. Dexter asked Mr. Benton if these sheep could be purchased. His reply was that they were on the way to market and he wouldn't have any objection to getting rid of them right then and there. Now Col. Dexter didn't know Mr. Benton but everyone for miles around knows about Col. James Dexter. Col. Dexter, who never wastes time haggling for a better price, asked Mr. Benton what he would get for the sheep at the market.

"Well someone told my foreman that they would bring five dollars a head," Mr. Benton told him.

"Okay, I'll give you five dollars a head if you would take them to the South Dakota border," Col. said. "I'll pick up the tab for the trip there."

Col. Dexter and Sister Susan Come Across a Little Nameless Town

Now Col. Dexter didn't have that kind of cash with him, but Mr. Benton was only too glad to trust Col. Dexter to send him the money when he returned to West Fork and the bank.

Once again, everyone was on their way but this time with a herd of three hundred prime sheep to help the residents in the little nameless town. (Col. Dexter and Sister Susan had gone on ahead and prepared the people for the big surprise.)

The next two days Col. Dexter and Sister Susan did wonders in helping the townsfolk raise their self-esteem and bring joy and hope to their houses. It was touch and go for a while. Dave told Col. Dexter that he left a few days earlier, and started looking for any kind of food they might have overlooked during their frame of mind. One of the residents remembered that he had buried some canned vegetables and fruit in an old root cellar at the end of the town in an old abandoned shack. They even found a cow stuck in some marshes that provided milk for the newborn twins. It's amazing how much clearer a person can think when he gets his mind off his own troubles and regains hope.

Col. Dexter and Sister Susan returned to Spencer just as the wagon train was coming over the rise. After a good night's rest, they once again headed for the little nameless town.

In appreciation for what he had done the townspeople voted and officially named the town Dexterville. And it is no longer a nameless town.

Pastor Wells was already primed for the return of the drovers and couldn't wait to tell what the Holy Spirit had dropped in his spirit for his Sunday sermon.

Pastor Wells told us that there wasn't anything that he could add because the Word had said it all. His only comment was that we can never go wrong if we take and apply to our heart the words found in the holy Scripture.

The Ol' Cowpoke gives thanks for his many blessings.

Below: Col. Dexter blesses the town with a means for survival.

CHAPTER 31

The Ol' Cowpoke Looks Up at the Three Crosses

And there were also two other, malefactors, led with him to be put to death. And when they were come to the place, which is called Calvary, there they crucified Him, and the malefactors, one on the right hand, and the other on the left.
And they found the stone rolled away from the sepulcher. And they entered in, and found not the body of Jesus. (LB)
—Luke 23:32-33, 24:2-3

Howdy saddle pals! We were on our way back to the Delta D with another new herd that we had bought at the market. This time I only took a dozen cowboys along with Blake, the trail cook. We were moving along fairly well when we noticed that the cattle were getting kinda restless. Matter of fact, they were real skittish. I got out Ol' Betsy my guitar from the chuck wagon and started to strum a tune. All the drovers began to hum along with my strumming, trying to settle the skittish cattle and keep them from getting frightened. Our herd was really larger than it should have been but I didn't want to wait for additional men to join us on the trail. We were still a long way from the ranch and I figured that we could handle them even though we were bringing back two thousand head which I bought at a super price. One of the cattle spread owners had taken this herd to sell because he had decided to get out of the cattle business and return to Washington State where he was needed to take over his father's business. The business had grown so large that his father could not continue control of the operation alone. I tried to hire some of the trail hands that had brought the cattle there but everyone wanted to take some much-needed rest. I really couldn't blame them but I surely could have used the help.

We were about three hundred miles from the Delta D and approximately seventy-five miles from any settlement or town. We were just sorta lumbering along when the cattle began to act like they could sense something unusual. Now cattle, as with any animal, instinctively can smell out trouble.

As we approached a rise on the otherwise flat ground, there seemed to be a mysterious and eerie glow just over the hill. It was just about sunset and I was getting nervous. More accurately, I was plain scared.

I decided to make it over the rise where we would set up camp for the night. I sent one of the drovers to accompany Blake and the chuck wagon on ahead to begin setting up camp. It would be at least an hour before we could join them.

About ten minutes had passed when all of a sudden I saw a rider coming over the rise in full gallop like something was after him. I noticed that when he got closer it was the rider I had sent with the chuck wagon. I had never seen a horse running as fast as he was traveling. I was somewhat concerned that he might spook the already nervous cattle and cause a stampede, so I coaxed Spirit into a gallop and met the rider before he got any closer.

Even in the near darkness I could tell that he was as white as a sheet. When I got him stopped he was speechless. I got the rider down off his horse and had him lie down. I worried that I might have a fainting man on my hands.

I finally got the rider settled down enough that he could begin to speak. I began questioning him about what had frightened him so. The rider's name was Banks Masters and he weighed about two hundred and twenty-five pounds. Now Banks was one who did not frighten easily. I was finally able to get some answers to my questions. I asked what had upset him so much and he gave his account of what was over the rise. Banks said that when he and Blake rode over the rise they were wondering what the glow was when all of a sudden they appeared. Banks started shaking and I was afraid he was having a seizure. He once again was speechless. Some water from my canteen calmed him once again.

I started to question him again and asked him point blank what it was that he had seen. Banks said that I wouldn't believe him. I told Banks to get a hold of himself and that I would believe him.

"We got over the rise and there in that ghostly glow were three crosses—just standing there in the wide open space," Banks explained.

I, too, became a little uneasy. I told the other cowboys to continue to push the herd along and that I was going to ride ahead with Banks to where the camp was being established.

Now when we got to the campsite, Blake didn't seem the least bit worried. He had gone ahead and set up the camp and had a good fire going. Sure enough, right there in the middle of nowhere stood three crosses. This vision reminded me of Christ's crucifixion. On the one in the middle hung a purple garment. On the top there was a crown of thorny branches. This, too, coincided with my recollection of Christ's death upon the cross.

Now Blake was one who had been around and had a wealth of knowledge from his travels.

"What do you believe made the eerie glow that we saw from over the ridge?" I asked.

He chuckled and pointed to the humus that had been placed at the foot of the crosses. "It is nothing but rotted wood shavings that the normal process of decay has caused. It is called phosphorous accumulation or phosphorescence.

"Now I can't tell where the crosses came from nor who put them there but I feel sure that someone human had done it."

It's too bad that Banks had built something into the sight that caused him to become so scared.

"Why I think that it is a beautiful sight and it reminds me that my Savior is not hanging on that old cross but is risen from the dead, praise God, and even now sits at the right hand of His Father."

Banks sure was relieved at the explanation and I believe that he got just a little bit closer to Jesus from this experience.

The next day after a great breakfast we broke camp and said goodbye to the crosses and started the herd moving. I believe that this really had a positive effect on the men and they will never forget the encounter with this unbelievable sight.

It took about three weeks to get back to the Delta D and everyone wanted to be the first to tell about our spiritual encounter.

I am never ceased to be amazed at Pastor Wells and how the Holy Spirit is always talking to him and we never get the chance to tell him things that we see on the trail. Ah! But I'm not complaining because you see as long as he is listening to the Holy Spirit then we all know that we are always getting the right stuff.

During his Sunday sermon, Pastor Wells looked up from his reading and asked the congregation, "Why wasn't He there?"

Everyone in the audience screamed out in unison, "He is risen! He is risen! Praise His Holy name!"

Well saddle pals, wasn't that a super story and as always keep your ears open and listening for "Howdy, saddle pals, this is the Ol' Cowpoke again with a brand new tale about the Old West." See you soon!

*The Ol' Cowpoke looks up
at the three crosses.*

The purpose of The Ol' Cowpoke Sez Howdy
is to reflect that
Jesus is the light of the world!